I0755875

QUARANTINE

QUARANTINE

How Saint Elizabeth Ann Seton Helped Me During the Early Months of the COVID-19 Pandemic

David von Schlichten

RESOURCE *Publications* • Eugene, Oregon

QUARANTINE
How Saint Elizabeth Ann Seton Helped Me During the Early Months of the COVID-19 Pandemic

Resource Publications
An Imprint of Wipf and Stock Publishers
199 W. 8th Ave., Suite 3
Eugene, OR 97401

www.wipfandstock.com

PAPERBACK ISBN: 978-1-6667-0057-2
HARDCOVER ISBN: 978-1-6667-0058-9
EBOOK ISBN: 978-1-6667-0059-6

05/25/21

For the Sisters of Charity
and for Mle.

Contents

Acknowledgments

Writing is always collaborative, even when it's not. Thank you to the students of my religious studies course on Seton. I am especially grateful for the feedback of the following students: Caitlin Wolfe, Andy Battaglia, Nicholas Rause, and Christy Gordon. I am also immensely grateful to the following colleagues who read the manuscript and gave me priceless feedback: Sister Colette Hanlon, Kendra McConnell, Dr. Nancy Raftery, Dr. Barbara Denison, Dr. Jen Jones, and Marissa Haynes. Katie Fitzpatrick, M.F.A. was a first-rate copy editor. I offer a special thank you to Dr. Catherine O'Donnell, the author of *Elizabeth Seton: American Saint* (Cornell University, 2018), an outstanding biography. Catherine graciously responded to emails from some scholar she never met by reading the manuscript and offering feedback.

I thank my wife, Kim von Schlichten, and my stepdaughter, Katie Ribblet, for letting me write about our home life.

Of course, thank you to Mle Jones, my granddaughter, for being such an uplifting and comforting person just by being herself.

Finally, thank you, Mother Seton, for everything.

1.

Introduction

When the COVID-19 Pandemic seized us here and it became clear that Seton Hill University in Greensburg, PA, where I teach, would have to go online for the rest of the spring semester of 2020, I connected to a key event in the life of our namesake, Saint Elizabeth Ann Seton (1774–1821), the first American-born person to be canonized (declared a saint) by the Roman Catholic Church and the foundress of the American Sisters of Charity of Saint Joseph. From November 19 to December 19, 1803, Mother Seton herself was forced into quarantine in Italy. She had traveled there in the hopes that the milder climate would help save her husband, William, who was sick with tuberculosis (called "consumption" back then). However, upon arriving from their home in New York City to Livorno, Italy, the Setons were forced into quarantine because the Italians feared that William was sick with the yellow fever ravaging New York at the time.

During that month-long struggle, Seton kept a journal, so two things occurred to me: 1. That keeping a journal myself during the COVID-19 Pandemic might be of benefit for future readers while also helping me cope; and 2. That reading and writing about Seton's own experience with keeping a journal during a quarantine might likewise be of benefit.

What you are about to read, then, is my journal that I kept during March, April, and May of 2020, when many of us were adjusting to social distancing, wearing masks, and working remotely. In this journal, I write about Seton's own journal and ordeal and connect her experience to my own. I hope that reading this provides you with comfort, wisdom, and points of connection for you mentally, emotionally, and spiritually.

Publishing a journal while I am still alive is tricky because, well, there is always more to write about. For instance, since my keeping of the journal, George Floyd has been horribly murdered by Derek Chauvin, a white police officer, and the nation is in the midst of what will hopefully be a seismic shift toward ending racism. In addition, the pandemic nightmare has gotten worse, despite there being a vaccine. Even so, I hope this brief snapshot is of value.

And there is more writing to come. There must be. I have no choice. I cannot help but write, and I wouldn't have it any other way.

Yours,
Dave
Monday, January 4, 2021
The bicentennial of Mother Seton's death

2.

The Weeds of Diaries/Journals

Getting into the weeds of diaries/journals is wild and something I've never explored much before this project. Throughout my life, I have kept a journal sporadically, but I rarely gave careful thought to the concept and features of a journal. For this project, I did some sustained thinking guided by research, particularly the work of journal scholars Margo Culley[1] and Philippe Lejeune.[2] My goodness, there's a lot to explore. I have barely begun.

We academics are often accused of overthinking things and making simple concepts unnecessarily complex. While there is probably some truth to those accusations (of course, I'll have to give them much, much more thought), they don't apply to diaries/journals.

First, which term do you go with, diary or journal? Many people indicate differences, such as that diaries are kept daily while journals are more sporadic, or that diaries are more personal. I've also seen scholars, such as Culley and Lejeune, use the terms interchangeably. Seton's work that I am exploring is generally called a journal, but it could just as easily be called a diary. Both are, to

1. For this book, I drew from Margo Culley, ed. *A Day at a Time: The Diary Literature of American Women from 1764 to the Present* (New York: Feminist, 1985).

2. For this book, I drew from Philippe LeJeune. *On Diary*, University of Hawaii Press, 2009. Jeremy D. Popkin, Julie Rak, Katherine Durnin, eds.

borrow from Lejeune's definition of diary, "a series of dated traces."[3] That is, both a diary and a journal are a series of dated entries. In this work, then, I am going to use mainly the word "journal" because Seton's work is often called by that term.

Second, a distinctive feature of a journal is that it is a genre a person writes in real time while in the midst of events. With other genres, including other non-fiction works about an individual's experiences (such as autobiography and memoir), the writer knows the outcome. Those works are written after the fact with the person looking back on what happened. But diaries are written now. In many works, the reader doesn't know what's going to happen next, but, in the case of a journal, the writer doesn't know, either.

That said, many diarists reread and revise their diaries, especially if the diarist has an audience in mind. If you revise your journal, are you somehow undermining the whole point of it, which is to capture a person's unfiltered thoughts and feelings in the moment? I have struggled with this issue in writing this journal for publication. I want it to reflect as authentically as possible my experience of the early months of the pandemic, but, at the same time, I want the journal to reflect well on my family and me and also be clear and accessible for a wide readership. My solution was to keep revisions to a minimum, but it's been challenging deciding what to revise.

Next, it's easy to plummet into existential bewilderment when writing a journal. Who will care about what I write? Why do I feel the need to express myself in writing? Why do I want an audience, a readership? Does the journal truly reflect the authentic me or some adulterated version? Do I even know what the authentic me is, and do I feel safe expressing that fully to anyone, let alone readers, some of whom I know well and some of whom I'll never meet? Can a person ever express the complete, authentic self without feeling a need to self-censor?

I don't fully know the answers to these questions, but my not knowing isn't going to keep me from writing. Indeed, my writing is integral to my thinking. I think; therefore, I write, and vice versa.

3. LeJeune, *On Diary*, 179.

The Weeds of Diaries/Journals

In considering Seton the diarist as creative writer, we find ourselves facing the journal-writing practices of her era. In Seton's day, it was common for men to keep diaries, which, contrary to the present-day understanding of this genre, was not a private document but one that was often at least semi-public.[4] Women, too, kept diaries, but, of course, women were generally less prominent than men, so their writings were less likely to find a public audience. Even so, a woman writer might still have in mind a reader, as Seton does in her Italian journal, which she wrote for her beloved sister-in-law, Rebecca Seton (whom she calls her "soul's sister").

During Seton's time, journals often functioned as a record of important events for other family members to read, and that is the case here. However, some journals kept only such a record with little commentary or expression of emotion. That is, journals were often merely a list of when babies were born, when people died, who got sick, what happened on the farm that day, and so forth. Seton's journal is more emotional and vivid.

It reminds me somewhat of the genre of spiritual autobiography, which recounts a person's journey from wretched sinfulness to faith in God. Of course, while it is clear from the beginning that Seton already has such faith firmly in place, we nevertheless see a spiritual journey. She and Anna reflect on their sinfulness and thus their need for God's grace. More notable is that we see Seton playing pastor to her (likely) dying husband, ensuring that his soul is right with God before he dies so that he goes to heaven. In ministering to her husband, who had been a fairly secular person for much of their marriage, Seton merges her identity as a wife with her identity as a Christian.[5] The spiritual journey, then, is hers as well as her husband's. As we will see, Seton's spirituality deepens during her time in the lazaretto, and it will continue to grow after she leaves and stays with the Filicchis, who will repeatedly try—with eventual success—to convert her to Roman Catholicism.

As Culley explains, women diarists often found through their writing an opportunity to construct the self. Culley notes that "[e]

4. Culley, *A Day at a Time*, 3.
5. O'Donnell, *Elizabeth Seton*, 122.

vidence abounds in all periods that women read and reread their diaries,"[6] that women diarists were aware of their audience, and that they constructed their journal persona with audience in mind.[7] Contrary to the popular notion that Seton simply scribbled down her thoughts and experiences without any filter or attention to audience, it makes more sense to surmise that she crafted this writing with at least Rebecca in mind. We will explore this possibility further a bit later.

In this book, I will not begin to do justice to the complexity of this underrated genre known as the journal. Even so, I hope my work here serves as a useful contribution to studies of Seton's Italian journal as a work of literature, and I hope my journal is useful for helping my readers through this pandemic.

Let us begin.

6. Culley, *A Day at a Time*, 13.

7. Culley, *A Day at a Time*, 10–11.

3.

Friday, March 20, 2020

Everyone's Gone

Everyone's gone. The students I adore—I live and work for them more than they know—are gone. The halls are empty. The doors are locked. We are open in that the school is up and running, but you'd never know it by walking around on campus. We are all hidden behind keyboards and screens.

A week ago today, the school where I work as a professor, Seton Hill University in Greensburg, PA, announced that classes would be online and that the university would be almost completely shut down. Students had to vacate dorms by today, although exceptions have been made for a handful of students, such as those from other countries who cannot return home. Only staff who must be on campus are here. Faculty are still allowed to work from their office, so I'm at mine. Most faculty, though, work from home. Food service continues, but we cannot eat in the dining hall. Classroom doors are locked. Meetings are virtual. I send videos to my students and post work for them to do online.

My last day in the classroom was Wednesday, March 11. I told the students that I didn't think we'd go online. Now, I won't be in a classroom with students until the start of the fall semester in August. Maybe not even then.

What will become of us?

How many will die? What other precautions will we take? I suspect that, in the next day or two, Pennsylvania governor Tom

Wolf will mandate that all of us stay home, just as we saw in California and New York.

We are a world of people trying to fight an enemy we cannot see and do not understand well. Anyone at any time could be infected, regardless of whether a person is presenting symptoms. Over 4,000 people have died in Italy, and we have heard repeatedly that the United States is following the same trajectory regarding the progression of the disease.

Are we doing enough? Are we overreacting? Am I safe? Is my family? My wife, daughter, and four-year-old granddaughter all live with me in Greensburg, PA, about a mile from Seton Hill—are we safe? My seventy-four-year-old stepdad who lives in eastern PA, my sister and her husband who live in New York, my brother who lives in New Jersey, my sister who is a nurse and lives in Arizona—are they all safe? How long will this go on?

The disease is spreading, the economy faltering. Some people are saying we are overreacting, but experts, such as Dr. Deborah Birx and Dr. Anthony Fauci, urge that we need to do more.

It all feels dystopian. Our world is lots of distancing and video meetings and avoiding each other, the exact opposite of how we humans generally prefer to interact. We are, on the whole, social creatures, so social distancing is profoundly against our natures, yet we have to do it in order to protect ourselves and one another.

What will become of us?

Mother Seton, pray for us.

It will surprise no one who knows me that I keep thinking of Saint Elizabeth Ann Seton (1774–1821), or Mother Seton, as she was known in her lifetime and as many of us still call her. The first American-born person to be canonized, she did not found Seton Hill but did found the American Sisters of Charity of Saint Joseph, who then founded Seton Hill in the late 1800s under the leadership of Mother Aloysia Lowe (1836–1889). Each morning, after making my way up the road that climbs the hill on which our campus sits, I pause at the white statue of tiny Seton (she was slender and scarcely five feet tall) and ask her to pray for us. I even chat with her a bit. Sometimes I imagine her responding, usually by giving a cheerful greeting or by urging me to be true to my principles and to be patient with the progress of my career and with life in general. She has continually been an inspiration and a fascination of mine since I started working here at Seton Hill full-time five-and-a-half years ago. I created a course about her, work her into every class I teach, have presented about her at conferences, and wrote an article and a book chapter about her. In May, two months from now, a colleague of mine and I were supposed to teach a version of my Seton course to a group of our students in Parma, Italy.

Much of life is no longer happening, at least for now, and nobody understands better what it is like to have disease put your life on hold than Mother Seton. In 1803, back when she was Elizabeth Ann Seton, the wife of William and mother of five children, she, like us, experienced rampant disease and had to be quarantined. She wrote about that crisis extensively in a journal. In fact, the journal was going to be the basis for our trip to Italy, since her experience of quarantine and disease and loss (and then discovery) all happened there.

A couple days ago, the obvious occurred to me: Seton's experience with disease and quarantine in Italy can resonate profoundly with us today. I started making three-to-five-minute videos for Facebook in which I tell her story and read from her journal. I have posted twice so far and am planning on posting twice a week for the next few weeks. The response has been positive. People are interested and encouraging, so, I thought, let's write some of this down.

All of this, of course, is a coping strategy on my part, a way of finding order and purpose and sense during this long, slow-burning nightmare that is unlikely to end any time soon.

I hope that you, like my viewers, will find enjoyment and inspiration in what I have written. If I get out of Seton's way, you will no doubt find both and more.

4.

Background on Saint Elizabeth Ann Seton and Her Italian Journal

Born Elizabeth Bayley in 1774, she married the wealthy William Seton in 1794 and had five children with him. These were the years of her life long before she converted to Roman Catholicism (1805) and founded the American Sisters of Charity of Saint Joseph (1809), which, under her leadership, ran a school for girls that was free for those who could not afford to pay. Back in the 1790s, Elizabeth Seton was a devout Episcopalian who lived happily in New York City with William and their five children, hobnobbing with the likes of the Hamiltons, until William's business went bankrupt and William contracted tuberculosis. Desperate for a recovery, William, Elizabeth, and their oldest daughter, Anna, who was eight, sailed across the ocean with the intent of staying with the Filicchis, a wealthy and devoutly Roman Catholic family in Livorno (Seton—unfortunately—calls it by the anglicized version of its name, "Leghorn") who were friends and business associates of William. The hope was that the milder weather might be conducive to William's recovery.

Elizabeth Seton kept a journal of the entire trip.

Upon arriving in Livorno in November, the Setons were informed by the Italians that they would have to be quarantined in a lazaretto. Named for the poor beggar "Lazarus" from the parable in Luke 16:19–31, lazarettos took different forms throughout history, but, in this case, it was a building in a canal near Livorno. We know from Seton's description that it was a spartan, cold, and dank room, little better than a prison. A mattress and a few other rude furnishings were brought in for the Setons, and a fire was built in the fireplace, although the smoke aggravated William's coughing. While they were originally to stay the standard forty days (the word "quarantine" comes from the Italian word for "forty days," *quarantina*), the Setons received a reduction to thirty days.[1] Even so, conditions were difficult, and, overall, William's health continued to decline. When they were released on December 19, they went to Pisa to stay in better accommodations arranged by the Filicchis, but it was too little too late. On December 27, William died.

William's death marks the end of what I call the "lazaretto portion" of the Italian journal. After William's death, there is a clear break. The second portion of the journal tells of Seton and Anna's time with the Filicchis, with whom they stayed until April. Seton wanted to journey home sooner, but obstacles kept delaying their departure, such as Anna contracting scarlet fever and a storm damaging their ship. During that time, the Filicchis introduced Seton to Roman Catholicism, with which she fell in love. Less than a year after returning home to the United States, she converted, even though doing so meant having to endure the anti-Catholic prejudice prevalent in parts of the United States.

In short, Seton's five months in Italy profoundly changed her life and so is historically significant for, not just Roman Catholics, but the burgeoning American nation. She would eventually be one of the great pioneers of Catholic education in America, and the

1. There is disagreement about how long the Setons were to stay in quarantine and how much they actually stayed. Some sources say they were initially to stay thirty days but were released after twenty-five. However, the journal makes clear that they were admitted on November 19 and released on December 19, which is thirty (or thirty-one, depending on how you count) days. Further, we find Seton reporting in her journal that their quarantine was shortened by five days (November 20) and then five more days (November 24). So, I agree with Barthel, who, in her biography of Seton (53), writes that the Setons were to be quarantined for forty days (the traditional length of a quarantine) but that their time was reduced to thirty.

work of her Sisters would span the world. She was canonized on September 14, 1975.

Even though Seton left behind many writings, I will focus here on the Italian journal, and only the lazaretto portion, since that is the part that has the most to say to us who are living through the COVID-19 Pandemic of 2020. Indeed, as you will see, the Italian journal is richly poetic and engaging, full of poignancy, vivid description, and wisdom. It is a remarkable work that deserves careful reading and study, not only because it was written by the great Seton, and not even only because it speaks to our current crisis, but because it is a beautiful, touching, and profound literary work.[2]

In reflecting on her journal, I suggest that it contains at least five themes. The first is that the journal features "hopeful honesty." Repeatedly, Seton is honest about how bleak her situation often is in the lazaretto. She writes of crying and of the distress of her family and of the dank and spare conditions in what was essentially one small step up from a prison. At the same time, she is ever hopeful, trusting in God (or "Providence," a favored term of hers). She would maintain this hopeful honesty throughout her life.

My second suggestion is that the journal features spiritual growth. Seton is clearly refining her sense of self. She is exploring having moments of doubt, how to relate to the people around her, especially her husband, and ultimately growing spiritually in a way that will benefit her many times throughout her life. Indeed, Seton scholar and Daughter of Charity Betty Ann McNeil writes that, for Seton, ". . . this time was a crucible of purification for spiritual growth."[3] Specifically, we will see that Seton matures during her ordeal in the lazaretto in that she learns how to grow spiritually stronger in response to hardship and in that, as Catherine O'Donnell astutely points out in *Elizabeth Seton: American Saint*, she unites her life as a Christian with her role as a wife.

Third, I suggest that Seton's journal features encountering the sacred in others. Repeatedly, Seton draws from and contributes to relationships as an integral part of her spirituality.

2. There are two versions of the journal, but the differences are not significant.

3. McNeil, *15 Days of Prayer*, 4.

Fourth, the journal highlights Seton's skill as a creative writer, something readers often overlook. In the case of the Italian journal, I do not mean that Seton is a creative writer in that she is producing fiction or poetry. I mean that she is using literary devices and techniques to craft an aesthetically compelling and even beautiful work of creative non-fiction. While not all her writing is artistically remarkable, the journal is. Amid the sometimes-awkward syntax and punctuation—Emily Dickinson was not the only one who loved the dash; actually, many nineteenth century writers did—we find one poetic and profound phrase after another, as well as rich descriptions and deep emotional and spiritual expression. I would rank Seton's journal with other great journals from American literature, including Thoreau's *Walden*, in part because of the beauty and profundity and poignancy, and in part because of the historical and cultural significance of Seton herself, who would go on to be one of the architects of Catholicism in America. Her journal is worthy of being taught in English classes and included in anthologies of American literature.

By the way, as I quote the journal, you will see numerous spelling mistakes, "unconventional" grammar, and capitalizations that we wouldn't do today. I chose not to "correct" Seton's writing but just to leave it as is.

Actually, given that Seton demonstrates elsewhere in her writing that she can be more polished and proper grammatically and given that diarists often revised their work, I wonder if Seton intentionally left her journal somewhat grammatically messy, perhaps as a way of highlighting her distress. In any event, the alleged errors are part of the work, as some of my students have noted. Actually, a few of them commented in my class on Seton that the errors helped to humanize the great saint. Even Saint Elizabeth Ann Seton, one of the pioneers of Catholic education in America, sometimes misspelled words.

My fifth suggestion about Seton's journal is that it has a strong mystical component. What do I mean by "mystical"? The word "mysticism" is often defined as union with God that is usually obtained through disciplines such as fasting and meditation and includes experiences such as visions. However, leading mysticism-scholar

Bernard McGinn contends that mysticism is better understood as an experience of "the immediate or direct presence of God,"[4] rather than as union or oneness with God. Similarly, Ronald Rolheiser contends that mysticism is "being touched by God at a level deeper than words, imagination, and feeling" that mystics, nevertheless, attempt to verbalize to some degree.[5] This focus on an extraordinary encounter with God is really more properly the focus of mysticism than oneness or unity with God, although oneness or unity may be part of the mystical experience.

Further, mystics tend to color outside the lines (or at least awfully close to the outside) of mainstream theology and frequently attempt to express their experiences in vivid, poetic fashion. Saint Hildegard of Bingen, Julian of Norwich, and Saint Teresa of Avila (in whom Seton took great interest) all spring to mind. Julian of Norwich's *Revelations of Divine Love*, which she wrote when Europe was reeling from the Bubonic Plague and was engaged in the Hundred Years' War, is a particularly powerful introduction to mystical writing. In any case, I suggest that at least the lazaretto portion of the Italian journal is mystical.

Given Seton's circumstances, it makes sense that we would see a pronounced mysticism in this portion of the journal. Mystical writings often emerge from people involved in crisis and/or engaging in prolonged acts of asceticism (acts of self-denial for spiritual purposes), prayer, meditation, and contemplation. Consider, again, Julian of Norwich, who had her visions during a period of severe illness and who spent much of her adult life confined to one room as an anchoress. Similarly, Seton is confined to a small space where she is clearly being deprived of basic comforts (and thus, by default, is experiencing asceticism) and is, by her own admission, frequently engaged in prayer, and meditation. The ordeal was ripe for mystical experiences, which Seton had repeatedly.

The study of mysticism is vast and complex, and I do not begin to do it justice here. Even so, I think I am right to suggest that there

4. McGinn, *The Presence of God*, xvii.

5. Rolheiser, "Introduction." John Markey and J. August Higgins, eds. *Mysticism and Contemporary Life*, 4.

is indeed a mystical component to the lazaretto portion of Seton's Italian journal that most readers have overlooked.

In fact, the mystical component and the creative writing component go together because mystical writers, in their efforts to express in words their experiences, are often highly poetic. Such is certainly the case here.

By the way, if you would like to read a copy of the journal, you can find it in its entirety for free at via.library.depaul.edu in Volume One of *Elizabeth Bayley Seton: Collected Writings*, edited by Regina Bechtle and Judith Metz (New City Press, 2000), starting on page 246. This is the source I used for studying the journal (unfortunately, because of the pandemic, I was unable to visit the archives in Emmitsburg to see the actual journal. Someday!)

5.

What's She Up To?

The Structure of the Lazaretto Portion of the Journal

While many readers of the Italian journal think this is just a spontaneous, unfiltered outpouring of Seton's thoughts and feelings in real time, the truth is likely more complicated. As I indicated, writers often edited their journals.

A closer examination reveals an intriguing structure to at least the lazaretto portion of the Italian journal that suggests planning and editing on Seton's part. For starters, this lazaretto portion begins twelve days before the quarantine starts and ends eight days after. In other words, the time in the lazaretto is bookended with events leading up to quarantine and events following quarantine, suggesting an intentional structure. The central event is, of course, William's declining health and death. So, the journal starts with hope about William's health, features the time in the lazaretto, and ends with his death. The Filicchi portion of the journal deals with Seton's movement toward Catholicism, but the lazaretto portion is primarily about Seton trying to save her husband.

Another feature of the lazaretto portion is that the opening entries focus on Anna, who, with her amazing piety, represents perfect faith. In the second half of the lazaretto portion, Anna is mentioned far less often. By contrast, while Seton focuses on William throughout the journal, during the last several entries she is intensely fixated on her less devout husband because he is dying and she is concerned about the state of his soul. So, we have a beginning that is hopeful and highlights the pious Anna, and we have a contrasting ending that is also hopeful but darker because William is dying and thus there is an urgent effort to ensure that he will go to heaven.

Another striking feature of the lazaretto portion's structure is the mystical component. The first entry contains a dream. So does the last entry. These dreams contain imagery and a focus on harmony with God reminiscent of mystical language. In the middle of the lazaretto portion is the December 1 entry, which is rich with imagery and language of unity with God and spirituality that reminds me of mysticism. I will go into detail on this entry later. My point, for now, is that the book has a heavy emphasis on mystical language at the beginning, center, and end of the journal, suggesting Seton's emphasis of her mystical side as a way of reassuring herself and her reader that God is guiding this entire ordeal toward a positive outcome.

This structure of the lazaretto portion of the journal suggests intentional artistry on Seton's part. This isn't something she just dashed off; it is something she worked on carefully. However, even if we cannot prove that she was being intentional, the patterns are there nonetheless, thus pointing to a complexity of the work that readers have generally overlooked.

6.

Her First Journal Entry

Tuesday, November 8, 1803

"*Was climbing with great* difficulty a Mountain of immense height and blackness when near the top, almost exhausted a voice said—'Never mind take courage there is a beautiful green hill on the other side—and on it an angel waits for you.' (at that moment Willy woke me to help him)"[1] This is how Seton begins her journal to her beloved sister-in-law, Rebecca. On this date, Seton, her husband, William, and their oldest daughter, Anna, were still traveling on the *Shepherdess* from their home in New York City to stay with the Filicchis in Livorno, Italy, not knowing that, upon arrival, she and her family would be forced into quarantine.

Before we proceed with reflecting on that first entry, it is important to say a word about Seton's relationship with Rebecca, her intended audience. Rebecca Mary Seton (1780–1804) was the second child of William Seton, Sr. (1746–1798) and his second wife, Anna Maria Curson Seton (1756–1792) and so was Seton's husband's half-sister. The woman Seton called her "soul's sister" was "meek"[2] and someone Seton tried to shape spiritually. For instance, she encouraged Rebecca to "skip family events rather than miss Sunday Communion"[3] and to take up spiritual readings such

1. Bechtle and Metz, *Collected Writings*, vol. I, 246. Here, there is a note added by the editors: "[at this point, the page is torn]"

2. O'Donnell, *Elizabeth Seton*, 101.

3. O'Donnell, *Elizabeth Seton*, 101.

as sermons.[4] Indeed, Seton, exhibiting leadership qualities early on, proceeded long before becoming a Sister to guide other women spiritually, "creating an informal spiritual sisterhood with herself as leader and gatekeeper."[5] At the same time, Seton confided her fears and sadness to Rebecca, such as when she admitted to her that she "cannot sleep" due to witnessing the high number of sick and dying immigrants that her physician father was tending to in New York in 1801.[6] Even so, she expressed to Rebecca that the dying infants of the crisis have "a provider in Heaven."[7] So, while Seton saw herself as a spiritual mentor for Rebecca, she also considered Rebecca someone she could confide in, at least to an extent.

There were clearly some points that Seton did not wish to disclose to Rebecca. For instance, while Seton wrote a letter to Antonio Filicchi in which she professes romantic feelings for him, she (understandably) makes no explicit mention of such feelings in her journal to Rebecca. So then, a question that hovers over the entire journal is: "How candid is Seton being?" How much of her writing is being shaped by her calling to be a spiritual guide for Rebecca as well as by her awareness that she is writing to her husband's half-sister?

I wish I could ask Seton directly. In fact, I often wish I could talk to her directly. Actually, I do talk with her almost every day in my imagination. Picturing that statue of her in front of our administration building at Seton Hill, I ask her to help us through the pandemic, help Seton Hill to prevail through this painful time, watch over my loved ones, and empower me to spread her legacy. Then I conclude by saying that, what I really want is for her to pray for me. (I then pray a "Hail Mary," even though that's not addressed to Mother Seton. It seems fitting somehow, maybe because Mother Seton had such a strong devotion to Mary.)

4. O'Donnell, *Elizabeth Seton*, 102.
5. O'Donnell, *Elizabeth Seton*, 102.
6. O'Donnell, *Elizabeth Seton*, 103.
7. Qtd. in O'Donnell, *Elizabeth Seton*, 103.

So, I talk to her a good bit, but regarding how much of her journal-self is a construction and how much of it is just her unfiltered, I receive no answers.

I do know, though, that how she chooses to start her journal to Rebecca fits well with the theme of hopeful honesty, this combination of frankness about suffering and faith in God. Seton begins with a dream about climbing a mountain and being reassured that, on the other side, will be comforting rewards of greenery and an angel. This imagery calls to mind many a poem as well as allegories such as John Bunyan's *Pilgrim's Progress* (1678), with which Seton almost certainly would have been familiar given its popularity in America and given how well-read she was. The image of climbing a mountain being associated with spiritual challenge shows up over and over in literature, as does the promise of reward upon completing the climb. Dante's vision of purgatory in the *Divine Comedy*, for example, is that of climbing a mountain.

This also introduces the theme of spiritual struggle as part of Seton's growth. In the lazaretto part of the journal, Seton labors to preserve her own faith while working to ensure that her husband, who had never been particularly religious until recently, will go to heaven if he dies. In the second half of the journal, when she is in Livorno with the Filicchis, her spiritual struggle is with discovering Roman Catholicism and moving away from the Protestantism with which she grew up.

Along with this struggle is faith in the promise of reward and comfort. Throughout the journal, Seton openly expresses pain about the struggle while also conveying confidence that God will help her and that her labors in the Lord will not be in vain. She is hopefully honest.

This combination of spiritual struggle and ultimate faith in God being present in this journal helps to correct a common misperception that Seton was not devoutly religious until the Filicchis introduced her to Roman Catholicism. For instance, the made-for-TV 1980 film about Seton, *A Time for Miracles*, suggests that Seton was not particularly devout until her time with the Filicchis. The early scenes in the film before the lazaretto make almost no mention of Seton's faith. When she is staying with the Filicchis, she is portrayed as being both drawn to and troubled by the "unquestioning faith" of that pious family. In reality, Seton was always inclined toward deep religious piety. For instance, she and Rebecca used to hop from church to church on Communion Sundays (remember that she was Protestant then and so did not receive weekly communion) so as to partake of the Sacrament as much as possible.[8] On her journey to Italy, she took with her a Bible, commentaries, Thomas à Kempis's spiritual classic *The Imitation of Christ*, and a collection of sermons by her pastor, John Henry Hobart. Repeatedly in the journal she writes of God and prayer. There is no doubt that she was a pious Christian long before the Filicchis introduced her to Roman Catholicism. At the same time, the spiritual struggle motif in the journal shows us that even saints—maybe especially saints—are no strangers to grief and doubt. As Catherine O'Donnell notes repeatedly in *Elizabeth Seton: American Saint*, Seton had periods of "spiritual dryness."[9] This opening dream imagery from November 8 also introduces the mystical theme. The journal repeatedly features dreams, imaginary encounters, talk of angels, and sublime experiences in worship that all call to mind mysticism.

Indeed, some have claimed that Seton, in general, was a kind of mystic. Betty Ann McNeil uses the word to describe Seton.[10] Joan Barthel asks in her 2014 biography of Seton, *American Saint: The Life of Elizabeth Seton*:

> Was she a mystic? If being a mystic means having an emotional experience of God, completely shutting out the world, having visions and miraculous happenings, she was not. If being a mystic means being constantly—*constantly*—aware of the presence of God in her life, going beyond spiritual reading and vocal prayer to a deep basking in the grace and love of God, then she was.[11]

Barthel's understanding of mysticism calls to mind the great twentieth-century Catholic theologian, Karl Rahner, who famously

8. Barthel, *American Saint*, 68.
9. O'Donnell, *Elizabeth Seton*, 118.
10. McNeil, *15 Days of Prayer*, xxvi.
11. Barthel, *American Saint*, 126.

averred, "... the devout Christian of the future will be a 'mystic,' one who has 'experienced' something, or he will cease to be anything at all,"[12] meaning that Christians need to encounter God profoundly in the everyday. In this sense at the very least, Seton was definitely a mystic, even if it might be—might be—a stretch to call her a mystic in the sense of figures such as Saint Teresa of Avila. In any case, there is clearly a mystical flavor to the lazaretto portion of the Italian journal, and perhaps careful study of other works of Seton will reveal a similar flavor. In other words, it may be that Seton was a mystic, but, here, I am simply making the case that the lazaretto portion of the Italian journal is mystical, and we can taste that mysticism in this first entry.

Next, this opening dream in her November 8 journal entry underscores that she will be repeatedly caring for her husband, of course. Beyond that, though, it points ahead to the importance of relationships all throughout the journal. Over and over, Seton wrote about key people, some of whom posed challenges for her but most of whom helped her. From her daughter, Anna; to the *Capitano* of the lazaretto; to Louie, an elderly assistant who cooked for them; to the Filicchis; Seton wrote at length about the many people who stepped up to guide her through her spiritual struggle and complemented her mystical experiences. She encountered God through other people, including her husband.

These relationships, as we will see, are crucial to Seton's hopeful honesty and spiritual growth. Throughout the journal, she indicates how other people help her to find hope and growth by providing her with comfort and strength.

Finally, this initial entry displays Seton's skill with words. While her writing is sometimes confusing and not always particularly engaging (is anyone's writing *always* engaging?), throughout much of her work we see a strong inclination for imagery and artful phrasing (as we often observe in the writings of mystics). She was a profoundly influential figure who helped to shape Christianity and education in America, and her writing more often than not rises to

12. Rahner, *Theological Investigations*, trans. Edward Quinn, 15.

an artistic level worthy of scrutiny and appreciation by scholars of American literature.

Clearly, then, this opening entry from November 8, like many beginnings of great works of literature, encapsulates major themes of this work to come. In a way, this initial entry is the entire journal in miniature.

7.

Monday, March 23, 2020

Bad is Here, Worse is Coming

Things fall apart. The rough beast slouches toward us. We are in "bad" with "worse" coming, moving toward us with gaining momentum. The stock market continues to tumble. Unemployment climbs. The pandemic spreads. Here in the United States, over 30,000 people have tested positive and over 400 have died. In Italy, over 5,000 have died. In Spain, over a thousand. Congress continues to bicker over the relief package, which will cost somewhere around two trillion dollars. The president leads in a way that suggests he is more concerned about his own advancement than about what is good for the nation.

And all of this is going to get markedly worse before it gets better.

This past weekend was our first one in which we basically stayed home the entire time because most businesses are closed and because we are supposed to stay home as much as possible. I get why, and I accept the need to make the sacrifice. I think of people throughout history who have had to make far greater sacrifices for the common good: people who surrendered their lives, or who had to go into hiding or hide others, or who had to survive without basic needs and face poverty and violence for the sake of others. Yes, we humans have a long history of rising to dire occasions with remarkable acts of self-sacrifice. Now is such a time, although, frankly, what many of us are called to is not nearly as great as what countless others have had to forbear. My call, at least for now, is basically to stay home as much as possible and to avoid close contact with others. That's a fairly small sacrifice. And I don't have to worry much about money. Kim's and my jobs are secure—at the moment—and we have extra right now because of our income tax returns.

So, we have it pretty good, at least today, but the weekend was still rough. It will take some getting used to, being home with my family, which includes Kim, my twenty-seven-year-old daughter Katie, and her daughter Mle, who is four. We also have seven cats and a greyhound, so that's a lot of mammals under one roof. Family—we love them, but oh, how they can drive us crazy! Especially for us introverts who have a painful need for rejuvenating alone time, which, oddly enough, is scarce in this world of social distancing. Right now, my life is of two extremes socially. I am either at work, where I have gone from many interactions throughout the day with colleagues I adore and students I love to sitting alone for hours—a solitude not very satisfying—or I am at home, where there is no escape from my family, whom I love, of course, but whom I need some distance from now and then, just as I am sure my family needs distance from me.

I wonder how Mother Seton handled that combination of isolation and inseparability that a person finds in quarantine.

8.

Her Arrival at the Lazaretto

The Shepherdess arrived at Livorno on November 18, 1803. The next day, November 19, the Setons learned that they would have to be quarantined. Seton wrote to Rebecca,

> —It was now explained that our ship was the first to bring the news of yellow fever in New York which our want of a Bill of Health discovered, that the Pilot who brought us in the Mole [the port] must lose his head, our ship must go out in the Roads and my poor William being ill must go with his Baggage to the Lazaretto—at this moment the band of music that welcomes strangers came under our cabin windows and played, "hail Columbia" and all those little tunes that set the darlings singing and dancing at Home—[1]

Note the irony she highlights of the band welcoming them as they learn that they must be quarantined, a small but significant example of Seton's literary skill.

She goes on to recount that she, William, and Anna were led by a guard who pointed the way with his bayonet[2] up twenty stone steps to No. 6.[3] She recalls that, "when we entered our room Anna

1. Bechtle and Metz, *Collected Writings*, vol. I, 249–50.
2. Bechtle and Metz, *Collected Writings*, vol. I, 252.
3. Bechtle and Metz, *Collected Writings*, vol. I, 252.

viewed the high arches, naked walls, and brick floor with streaming eyes."[4] The Setons were provided with mattresses to lie on and then were "bolted and barred . . . in this immense place alone for the night."[5] The Capitano, the military man in charge of the lazaretto (curiously, not a physician), sent eggs, wine, and bread, but William, at least, didn't touch any of it that first day.

These descriptions of the lazaretto and the Setons's initial experience in it are striking for several reasons. The vividness of the description, including Seton recounting Anna's and her tears, is quite moving. It's hard not to sympathize with this family that came to Italy expecting the comfort of wealthy friends in the hopes that it would help to save William's life. Seton, clearly distraught, recalls, "I had heard the Lazaretto the very place for comfort for the sick . . . soon found there was a little closet, on which my knees found rest, and after emptying my heart and washing the bricks with my tears returned to my poor Willy."[6] A few lines later, she confesses, "my eyes smart so much with crying, wind and fatigue that I must close them and lift up my heart—sleep wont [sic] come very easily."[7] As Anna clings to her mother and sobs, Seton reads to her. Anna then says, "'Mamma if Papa should die here—but God will be with us,'" which Seton follows with a reflection to herself: "—God is with us—and if sufferings abound in us, his Consolations also greatly abound, and far exceed all utterance—."[8] Thus, in a few lines we see a poignant example of Seton's literary skill in capturing the pathos of a scene. She describes the spare, bleak conditions, the act of praying, food provided, and an exchange with Anna, thus engaging multiple senses in a way that immerses the reader in the moment. This scene also exemplifies Anna's identity throughout the lazaretto portion of the journal as the champion of the faith, even while she is grieving their plight. Further, we see in these lines Seton's hopeful honesty. She is frank about the pain of their situation. Her eyes hurt

4. Bechtle and Metz, *Collected Writings*, vol. I, 248.
5. Bechtle and Metz, *Collected Writings*, vol. I, 248.
6. Bechtle and Metz, *Collected Writings*, vol. I, 253.
7. Bechtle and Metz, *Collected Writings*, vol. I, 253.
8. Bechtle and Metz, *Collected Writings*, vol. I, 253.

from crying, and she admits, through the inclusion of Anna's statement, that her husband might not survive. Even so, she expresses trust that God's consolations will match their sufferings, even to the point of "far exceed[ing] all utterance."[9] The next day is no better. On the morning of November 20, which Seton indicates is a Sunday (and thus a day for going to church, which she cannot do), she writes that "The Matin Bells [bells announcing morning prayer] awakened my Soul to its most painful regrets and filled it with an agony of Sorrow which could not at first find relief even in prayer."[10] This moment is striking because it shows Seton admitting to an instance of spiritual faltering. Prayer, which she relied on continually, afforded her no relief. These moments of spiritual dryness recurred throughout her life, despite her great piety. For instance, she had such a spell when pregnant with her youngest child, Rebecca, who, at the time of the journal, was little more than a year old.

On November 20, while in the lazaretto, what seemed to break Seton from that instance of dryness was the ocean. After confessing to not finding relief in prayer, she indicates that:

> In the little closet from whence there is a view of the Open Sea, and the beatings of the waves against the high rocks at the entrance of this Prison which throws them violently back and raises the white foam as high as its walls, I first came to my senses and reflected that I was offending my only Friend and resource in my misery and voluntarily shutting out from my Soul the only consolation it could recieve [sic].[11]

In this stunning description, the ocean is fierce, violent, and spews white foam as high as the "prison" walls. Several times in the journal, Seton connects storms and the ocean with the power of God, and she seems to do so here, since, after observing the ocean's power and fury, she "came to [her] senses" and realized that she was "offending" her only Friend and resource, that is, God, and shutting her soul from God's comfort. She goes on to say that "pleading for

9. Bechtle and Metz, *Collected Writings*, vol. I, 253.

10. Bechtle and Metz, *Collected Writings*, vol. I, 254.

11. Bechtle and Metz, *Collected Writings*, vol. I, 254.

Mercy and Strength brought Peace," and then she focuses on tending to William with a "chearful [sic] countenance."[12] In this case, at least, what liberates her from her moment of struggling faith is nature reminding her of God's wrath, as well as the promise of God's healing mercy. Hence, she writes of "offending" God and then "pleads" for mercy and strength.

Throughout her life, Seton expressed her unworthiness and weakness as a human and therefore her need for God. Indeed, she thought such was the case for all of humanity. Humans are horribly inadequate except by God's magnanimous grace. She also repeatedly worried a bit about the wrath of God while mainly trusting in God's mercy.

She goes on to write of the unpleasant conditions in the lazaretto, such as the cold bricks and, when there is a fire, the smoke, which aggravates William's cough. She writes of William's recurring "ague" (fever) that leaves him "shivering and groaning."[13] The lazaretto was mainly a place of unrelenting sorrow and pain for her.

But then, that theme of hopeful honesty always recurs, sometimes in humbling ways. For instance, on Monday, November 21, she explains that she "[r]ead and jumped the rope[14] to warm me looked round our Prison and found that its situation was beautiful,"[15] although it is unclear what about it was beautiful. She rubbed William's hands to warm them and wiped his tears while praying for him. Then "Ann" read, and Seton watched the sun set. After both Anna and William fell asleep, Seton "read prayed wept and prayed again till Eleven—at no loss to know the hours—night and day four Bells strike every hour and ring every quarter—."[16] That's where the entry ends. Perhaps, then, it was the combination of being with loved ones, praying, listening to the bells, and watching the sun set that made the situation beautiful.

12. Bechtle and Metz, *Collected Writings*, vol. I, 254.
13. Bechtle and Metz, *Collected Writings*, vol. I, 254.
14. I love the endearing image of Seton jumping rope.
15. Bechtle and Metz, *Collected Writings*, vol. I, 256.
16. Bechtle and Metz, *Collected Writings*, vol. I, 256.

Even more striking is that, on November 24, she declares, "I find my present opportunity a Treasure—and my confinement of Body a liberty of Soul which I may never again enjoy whilst they are united."[17] She is thankful for time with her religious books and her "nursing duty."[18] Perhaps she is welcoming the opportunity for some spiritual pruning. She indicates that "Ann" is "happy with her rag baby and little presents."[19] She also received news from the Capitano of the lazaretto that their quarantine would be shortened by five more days beyond the five mentioned on November 20, for a total of ten days. She struggled to comfort William until he fell asleep from fatigue, after which she describes once again a "heavy storm of wind which drives the spray from the Sea against our window adds to his Melancholy—if I could forget my God one moment at these times I should go mad—but He hushes all—Be still and know that I am God your Father—,"[20] this last phrase an allusion to Psalm 46:10: "Be still, and know that I am God."

In this scene, Seton expresses that her confinement is good for her spiritually. But then, she expresses a mixture of joy and sorrow before concluding with a confidence in God that seems to be a reaction to the brutal storm outside. Once again, the fierce natural conditions led her closer to God. In this case, though, nature did not remind her of God's wrath but instead was a force that prompted her to cling to God for comfort.

On December 4, she goes even further in seeing the bright side of her confinement. She writes of enjoying reading her religious books, including the Bible and commentaries on it, during which she sensed an angel present. She refers to this angel as a guardian one but then also calls it the angel of John Henry Hobart, her priest back home whose sermons she had with her. Of these times of quiet reading and contemplation she writes, "These hours I often think I shall hereafter esteem the most precious of my life."[21] As O'Donnell

17. Bechtle and Metz, *Collected Writings*, vol. I, 257.
18. Bechtle and Metz, *Collected Writings*, vol. I, 258.
19. Bechtle and Metz, *Collected Writings*, vol. I, 258.
20. Bechtle and Metz, *Collected Writings*, vol. I, 258.
21. Bechtle and Metz, *Collected Writings*, vol. I, 267.

suggests, "She was becoming a spiritual virtuoso, and the days in the lazaretto afforded endless hours to hone her skills."[22] McNeil makes the same point when she writes of this time in the lazaretto that it was "a crucible of purification for spiritual growth."[23]

We also see in this scene a reminder of what a concrete and relational theologian Seton was. She rarely dwelt in pure abstractions or in systematic theologizing. Her theology was in concert with her circumstances: the weather, the people around her, her work. For Seton, God's presence was all throughout her setting and interactions and spiritual labor. In this regard, then, we perceive her mystical side in the sense of one constantly aware of the presence of God. We also see in moments such as these her Eucharistic side (what I call her Eucharistic heuristic) in that she encountered God in the concrete, physical, and fleshly world. For her, God was present in the moment, among the people, in the weather, just as God is present in the bread and the wine. Although she did not believe in the Real Presence of the Eucharist at this point, we can see in this kind of theology how arriving at the belief would be fairly easy for her, as it indeed proved to be in the coming months.

Seton exemplifying her hopeful honesty, spiritual maturity, and mystical side through finding the sacred in the people and places and events swirling around her challenges me to go and do likewise, including during this time of pandemic. Sometimes, that is far easier said than done.

22. O'Donnell, *Elizabeth Seton*, 121.

23. McNeil, *15 Days of Prayer*, 4.

9.

Monday, March 23, 2020 Continued

Mle

Especially challenging, while also endearing, is my four-year-old granddaughter, Mle (pronounced "Emily"). Katie and M live with Kim and me, and that's fine. But M, for reasons not quite clear, has really latched on to me, so she wants to play with me almost constantly. Now, I enjoy playing with her and have a lot of stamina and childlike zaniness, but man, the days get long because it's nonstop.

We have her calling me "Opa," the German word for "Pappy" or "Grandpa." I love that she calls me that and Kim "Oma," but she summons me over and over and over all day long. Throughout the house, she shouts:

"Opa!"

"Opa!"

"*Opa!*"

All day long.

Sure, that's sweet. It is. I get that. And I get that much of the world is dealing with far more serious matters. But all day long? I can't leave the room or be out of her sight for more than a few seconds. In the lazaretto, Seton couldn't get away from her daughter and husband, except for when they slept or when she slipped off to the partial "closet" she mentions. Seton seemed to handle the demands of her family in close proximity much better than I handle mine, or at least that's how she presents herself in her journal. Then again, when Anna was three, about the same age M is now, Seton complained about how difficult she was to discipline.[1] Maybe a tyrannical toddler is trying for us all, saint or no.

Perhaps M is just being a typical four-year-old, but I still find myself wondering. I mean, sure, I'm fun to have around—I'm up for doing whatever she wants to do, whether it's belt "Let It Go" from *Frozen* or be Mle's patient so she can be my doctor and listen to my heart with one of her toy stethoscopes—but her need to be with me as much as she does seems to arise from something deeper than just that I am fun to play with or that she is four.

And then there are the bursts of meanness. Here, I recall again Seton's frustration with the temper of Anna when she was three. Yes, I understand that M is four, and who knows what stressors her young mind is battling with? The world is confusing and frightening to us adults. How much more so when you are four? So, I try to be patient when she suddenly tells me, "Opa, stop! You're being bad," and I have no idea what I've done wrong. She does this to all of us, actually, but it seems like I get it more than others.

She's also going through a phase of hitting us. Again, I know that young children struggle with controlling their emotions. I mean, don't we all? I certainly have, although, over the past eight years, my emotions have been largely under control. Largely. It is even harder for a young child to express emotions appropriately. So, the hitting I can understand, even if I disapprove. Kim and Katie understand, too. We keep working on strategies for how to deal constructively with the hitting. We know yelling doesn't work. Hitting back definitely doesn't work, and I wouldn't do it even if it did. I resolved a long time ago that hitting was not going to be an action I resorted to unless absolutely essential for my safety or survival.

You never need to hit a four-year-old for your safety or survival.

Yesterday, Mle hit me numerous times. She had hit others, too, but I got the impression that she was particularly focused on hitting me. A couple times I snapped at her to stop it and walked away from her. That probably wasn't the most constructive strategy, but I was fed up.

1. O'Donnell, *Elizabeth Seton*, 82.

The second time seemed to strike a chord with her. She had hit me four times in the space of two minutes.

"Stop hitting me!" I snapped, startling her. She walked away from me toward the steps and ascended them part way before stopping to stare at me, looking like she got that I meant business.

"I play with you all day, and you keep being mean to me," I said from the couch, where she had hit me. "It makes me mad, and it makes me sad. It makes me want to cry." I got up and walked out of the living room, through the dining room, and to our room in the back of the house. It's a den, I suppose, but we keep many of M's toys there and often just call it "The Back Room." I closed the door and sat in there on an old, orange chair, heart heavy.

The world's battling a pandemic. Our economy is crumbling. Our national leadership is curved in on itself. The students are just online presences. The halls of Seton Hill are ghostly. And now a four-year-old, whom I adore to a painful degree, hits me.

I need to be strong and mature for M, but I also need to take time to be sad and frustrated and hurt. She definitely shouldn't see some of that. We are not to force adult problems onto children. At the same time, perhaps it is acceptable to let Mle know that I am sad and angry about her hitting me so that she can grasp that actions have consequences.

I sat alone in the back room in the orange chair waiting for I wasn't sure what, trying to calm myself, soaking up some desperately needed alone time, maybe like Seton in her closet.

10.

Anna

Central to the lazaretto part of the Italian journal are, of course, Seton's daughter Anna and her husband, William. Neither figures prominently in the second part of the journal, but here in the lazaretto portion, they are central. I will start with Anna.

Let's explore further Anna's central role in the journal: as the embodiment of ideal piety. Without fail, she expresses passionate faith in God even while grieving their situation.

For example, in her entry for November 11, Seton writes,

> My dear little Anna shed many tears on <my> her Prayer book over the 92nd Psalm in consequence of my telling her that we offended God every day Our conversation began by her asking me "if God put down our bad actions in his Book as well as our good ones"—
>
> She said she wondered how any one [sic] could be sorry to see a dear baby die
>
> She thought there was more cause to cry when they were born.[1]

In this entry that Seton wrote on board the *Shepherdess* while traveling to Italy, she illustrates her own piety and the extraordinary, precocious piety of eight-year-old Anna. Indeed, Anna's sentiments here reflected Seton's own theology, including her hopeful honesty.

1. Bechtle and Metz, *Collected Writings*, vol. I, 247.

Throughout the journal and her life, Seton expressed tremendous humility and guilt over her shortcomings and sins while also throwing herself into the arms of God's grace. In fact, we hear her articulate just such a position a few lines beyond the quote above from Anna. Seton writes,

> Considering the Infirmity, and corrupt Nature which would overpower the Spirit of Grace, and the enormity of the offence [sic] to which the least indulgence of them would lead me—in the anguish of my Soul shuddering to offend my Adored Lord—I have this day solemnly engaged that through the strength of His Holy Spirit I will not again expose that corrupt and Infirm nature to the Smallest temptation I can avoid—and therefore if my Heavenly Father will once more reunite us all that I will make a daily sacrifice of every wish even the most innocent least they should betray me to a deviation from the Solemn and sacred vow I have now made—[2]

She goes on to implore God to "imprint" on her soul "the strength of thy Holy Spirit" so that she may be supported and never forget "that Thou are my all." She concludes with "O keep me for the sake of Jesus Christ," and on the next line writes, "Shepherdess—."[3] Seton (and Anna) humbles herself before God, full of a painful awareness of her sinfulness while also confident in God's grace.

This last word, incidentally, is intriguing for its poetic ambiguity. It was the name of the ship she was travelling on, yes, but could it also be a reference to Jesus Christ, whom she mentions in the previous line and who is often described as a shepherd? If that is the case, then she is feminizing Christ, a move that was certainly not unprecedented (Julian of Norwich, writing in the fourteenth century, describes Christ repeatedly as "mother," for example) but that was nevertheless unusual in Seton's day (and today). Following the prayer "O keep me for the sake of Jesus Christ" immediately with the word "Shepherdess" suggests that Seton is engaging in wordplay here, perhaps reflecting a proto-feminist impulse.

2. Bechtle and Metz, *Collected Writings*, vol. I, 247.

3. Bechtle and Metz, *Collected Writings*, vol. I, 247.

Whether Seton had such an impulse is highly debatable. Barthel writes Seton had a "feminist heart,"[4] while O'Donnell does not use the word "feminist" to describe her. In any case, the wordplay suggests that, once again, we are seeing Seton's literary talent at work.

We also may be seeing a subversive quality. Given that the *Shepherdess* was the name of her ship, the double-meaning could be a clever way of Seton being proto-feminist while also having an out should someone challenge her. Then again, Rebecca was the intended reader of this journal. Would Rebecca have cared if Seton had been subversive as a proto-feminist? It was common for women, in their writings to each other, to be more candid about their thoughts and feelings than their patriarchal culture allowed. Sadly, we have no record of how Rebecca responded to the journal, since she died shortly after Seton returned home to New York in June of 1804. Would Rebecca have responded positively or negatively to this bit of subversion? Maybe she wouldn't have noticed it. We don't know, and we don't know if Seton is being intentionally subversive here. What we do know is that the text, regardless of Seton's intentions, contains an intriguing double-meaning.

To return to Anna, we see several more instances of Seton capturing in words her daughter's exceptionally mature devotion to God. On November 15, Seton, after her usual practice of reading and praying before bed and now struggling to sleep, heard "a little voice (my own Anna who I thought was asleep) in a soft wisper [sic] said 'Come hither all ye weary Souls'—I changed my place to her arms—the rocking of the vessel and breaking of the waves were forgot . . . ."[5] Anna comforted her mother by quoting an Isaac Watts hymn that was, in turn, quoting Matthew 11:28. In fact, Seton underscores this point by writing "—Adored Redeemer it was thy word, by the voice of one of thy little ones, who promises indeed to be one of thy Angels—."[6] Anna was angelic, a heavenly messenger drawing from the words of Jesus to help bring rest to her mother in

4. Barthel, *American Saint*, 138.

5. Bechtle and Metz, *Collected Writings*, vol. I, 248.

6. Bechtle and Metz, *Collected Writings*, vol. I, 248.

a moment that, with the voice and imagery floating on the edge of sleep, borders on the mystical.

Seton continues to describe Anna's religiosity. On November 22, she writes of Anna's dream about two men threatening her with a knife. When Anna awoke from the dream, she found comfort in her faith in Jesus.[7] On November 29, Seton recalls Anna worrying: "'one thing always troubles me mamma—Christ says they who would reign with Him must suffer with Him—and if I was now cut off where should I go for I have not yet suffered'—."[8] Seton indicates that Anna was coughing a lot, clearly sick herself (a haunting foreshadowing of Anna's later lethal bout with tuberculosis). Anna responded to her illness by saying "sometimes I think when this pain comes in my Breast, that God will call me soon and take me from this world where I am always offending him, and how good that would be, if he gives me a sickness that I may bear patiently, that I may try and please Him."[9] When Seton reassured Anna that she did indeed please God when she, Anna, helped her mother, Anna replied, "O do I Mamma thank GOD, thank GOD."[10] Anna, like her mother, felt unworthy before God and feared God's wrath but ultimately saw God as more merciful than wrathful. God responded to Anna's care for her mother by showing Anna mercy.

Wondering if Seton is exaggerating Anna's piety, I consulted Barthel's and O'Donnell's biographies for more information on this little girl. Is this construction of Anna part of Seton's construction of her journal-persona for Rebecca's edification?

From my reading, I have gleaned that, while Seton may have embellished a bit for Rebecca's benefit, Anna was, indeed, a pious child. O'Donnell is particularly insightful. She writes, "Possessed of a tempestuous nature mingled with a desire to please, Anna Maria reminded Elizabeth of her own younger self."[11] Even when Anna was only three, Elizabeth encouraged her daughter to improve her

7. Bechtle and Metz, *Collected Writings*, vol. I, 249.
8. Bechtle and Metz, *Collected Writings*, vol. I, 260.
9. Bechtle and Metz, *Collected Writings*, vol. I, 260–1.
10. Bechtle and Metz, *Collected Writings*, vol. I, 261.
11. O'Donnell, *Elizabeth Seton*, 82.

"moral character"[12] while also seeing in her "the Friend, Companion, and Consolation of my future years."[13] This statement suggests that Seton placed a tremendous amount of pressure on her daughter, a pressure, actually, she ended up regretting.[14] In any case, she was determined to secure an intimate bond with Anna and, overall, was successful.

Granted, Anna, as a young teenager, rebelled against her mother's religious life, spending time living in Baltimore, and also considered marrying a young man named Charles de Pavillon before he left her for another girl. Soon, though, Anna found herself missing Emmitsburg and returned to be with her mother, "rededicat[ing] herself to what had been her occupation most of her life: serving as boon companion to her mother."[15] Shortly before her death at age sixteen, she took vows to become a Sister of Charity. So, Seton's portrait of Anna being precociously devout and close to her mother is likely accurate.

12. O'Donnell, *Elizabeth Seton*, 82.

13. Qtd. on 82, O'Donnell, *Elizabeth Seton*.

14. Elizabeth Bayley Seton to Julia Scott, 20 September 1809, Bechtle and Metz, *Collected Writings*, vol. II, 84.

15. O'Donnell, *Elizabeth Seton*, 295.

11.

William

While Seton found comfort in her daughter's piety, she worried about her husband's salvation, and it was during their time in the lazaretto that, as O'Donnell points out, Seton's life as a Christian and life as a wife came together.[1] Seton's work with William was integral to her spiritual growth.

William, like Seton's father (and many men of that period), had not been particularly devout (until fairly recently). As William edged closer to death, Seton grew increasingly concerned about his soul. The lazaretto portion of this journal, then, is, in part, an account of Seton serving as her husband's pastor (a striking example of gender role-reversal), striving to ensure that, if he did die, he would enter eternal life, not eternal damnation. She writes often of his coughing and "ague," making clear that the cold, damp, and smoky air (from the fire they burned) were not conducive to William's recovery. Indeed, Seton and Anna both leaned toward believing that William would not survive. Anna said, on November 19, the day they entered the lazaretto, "'Mamma if Papa should die here—but God will be with us . . .'"[2] Thus, Seton's concern was trying to help him recover physically while also preparing him spiritually in the likely event that he would die soon. These words

1. O'Donnell, *Elizabeth Seton*, 122.
2. Bechtle and Metz, *Collected Writings*, vol. I, 253.

of reassurance are even more poignant and significant given that Seton wrote this journal for Rebecca, William's half-sister.

Repeatedly, she expresses that William's soul was in the right place but that he needed her pastoral guidance. She writes on November 30, "My Williams [sic] Soul is so humble it will hardly embrace that Faith which is its only resource."[3] Apparently, William was not trusting in God sufficiently. In fact, Seton addresses William a few lines later (although it does not appear that she literally said this line to William), writing, "Dear W it is not from the impulse of terror you seek your God, you tried and wished to serve him long before this trial came, why then will you not consider him as the Father who . . . will graciously recieve [sic] those who come to him . . . you say your only hope is in Christ what other hope do we need?—."[4] William resisted giving himself to God, much to Seton's concern. She goes on to recall William first being moved toward reforming himself spiritually upon hearing their pastor, John Henry Hobart, preach against materialism in favor of focusing on spiritual matters, especially the Gospel.[5] She also recalls that a business associate, "Mr. F.D." prompted shame in William by mentioning that, despite his (Mr. F.D.'s) material success, he praised God. Seton concludes, "These he called his two warnings which awakened his Soul—and speaks of them always with tears—."[6] Clearly, she indicates that, while William used to not care about spiritual matters, he had changed and now was attentive to them, even if there persisted a bit of hesitancy in him.

She continues to minister to her struggling husband. For instance, on December 1, she writes, ". . . often when he hears me repeat the Psalms of Triumph in God, and read St. Pauls [sic] faith in Christ with my Whole Soul, it so enlivens his Spirit that he also makes them his own . . . ."[7]

3. Bechtle and Metz, *Collected Writings*, vol. I, 261–2.
4. Bechtle and Metz, *Collected Writings*, vol. I, 262.
5. Bechtle and Metz, *Collected Writings*, vol. I, 262.
6. Bechtle and Metz, *Collected Writings*, vol. I, 262.
7. Bechtle and Metz, *Collected Writings*, vol. I, 265.

On December 13, she indicates somber relief over William's spiritual state, asserting,

> My heart used to be very full of poetical visions . . . but it has no room for visions *now*—one only vision is before it—No one ever saw my Willy without giving him the quality of an amiable man—but to see that character exalted to the Peaceful Humble Christian . . . is a happiness allowed only to the poor little Mother who is separated from all other happiness . . . .[8]

She also presents herself once again in the pastoral role for William when she writes a few lines later, "No sufferings, nor weaknesses nor distress . . . can prevent his *following* me daily in Prayer . . . ."[9] Further, William echoed Seton's recognition of the good of this dire situation. She writes on that same date, ". . . he very often says *this* is the period of his life which if he lives or dies he will always considered as Blessed . . . ."[10] On December 15, Seton reports that William ". . . feels like a person brought to the Light after many years of darkness when he heard the Scriptures as the law of God and therefore Sacred, but not discerning what part he had in them or feeling that they were the fountain of Eternal Life."[11] During his final hours, William magnified his fervor for God. On December 26, the day before his death, he called "his Redeemer to Pardon and release him."[12] Seton was by his side, continually repeating Scripture and prayer "which seemed to be his only relief."[13] He "felt so comfortable an assurance that his Redeemer would recieve [sic] him,"[14] even going so far as to say to Anna that he would take her with him if he could.[15] At four the next morning, he said, "'*My dear Wife and little ones*'" and "'*My Christ Jesus have mercy and recieve*

8. Bechtle and Metz, *Collected Writings*, vol. I, 269.
9. Bechtle and Metz, *Collected Writings*, vol. I, 269.
10. Bechtle and Metz, *Collected Writings*, vol. I, 269.
11. Bechtle and Metz, *Collected Writings*, vol. I, 271.
12. Bechtle and Metz, *Collected Writings*, vol. I, 274.
13. Bechtle and Metz, *Collected Writings*, vol. I, 274.
14. Bechtle and Metz, *Collected Writings*, vol. I, 274.
15. Bechtle and Metz, *Collected Writings*, vol. I, 274.

[sic] *me*."[16] Then he said, "'*my Christ Jesus*" until 7:15, when he died.[17] To underscore her confidence that William went to heaven, she writes on that same day, December 27, the day of his death, "My William often asked me if I felt assured that he would be accepted and pardoned, and I always tried to convince him that where the soul was so humble and sincere as his, and submission to Gods [sic] will so uniform as his . . . that it became sinful to doubt one moment of his reception through the merits of his Redeemer."[18] Even so, she confesses that, the night before his death, she prayed that God would pardon him and thus receive him into heaven.[19]

What can I learn from Seton's care for Anna and William? One lesson is a reminder of the care that children can provide us adults. Boundaries are important, of course. I do not want to put upon little Mle a responsibility to care for me that she is incapable of providing, but there are ways that she does indeed console and uplift all of us. Through her snuggling and playing and innocence, of course, she helps each of us. When I watch her work intently on something or be thrilled about the simplest pleasure, my heart feels renewed despite this harsh world full of painful breaths. It almost hurts to behold such innocence, but the joy is far greater than the heartache.

What other ways can children care for us adults? I'll keep pondering this.

What about my relationship with Kim and Katie? Mother Seton was caretaker and pastor for her husband. My wife and daughter, thank God, are not deathly ill like William, but they definitely have their challenges (as do I). How can we all support each other better?

Maybe one way is to identify what each of us needs the most help with. William needed help with his physical health and also his spiritual well-being and morale. Anna needed a bit of care for her health (when she became ill briefly in the lazaretto), and she also

16. Bechtle and Metz, *Collected Writings*, vol. I, 274.
17. Bechtle and Metz, *Collected Writings*, vol. I, 274.
18. Bechtle and Metz, *Collected Writings*, vol. I, 275.
19. Bechtle and Metz, *Collected Writings*, vol. I, 275.

needed emotional comfort from her mother. Elizabeth certainly leaned on Anna for emotional and spiritual support.

What do Kim, Katie, Mle, and I need from each other?

Mainly I need quiet time, validation, and empathy. I need reassurance that the others recognize my efforts and appreciate them, and I need expressions of understanding when I am feeling stressed or down. Really, Kim and Katie need the same thing. In addition, they both need assistance with simply getting things done. I need to help Kim better by pushing myself to do more around the house, and I continue to help Katie by caring for Mle. As far as Mle goes, she wants and needs play time, of course, as well as basic necessities and structure. But she also needs reassurance. That little girl worries a lot about her safety. For example, she is afraid that lawn mowers will hurt her and gets anxious whenever she hears one. That may seem silly or endearing, but it's neither to her. So, we tell her over and over that she is safe with us, that mowers will never harm her.

I'll keep pondering Mother Seton's caring for her husband and daughter (and *vice versa*).

12.

Friday, March 27, 2020

Stay-at-Home Order

Today Governor Wolf announced that our county, Westmoreland, PA, is under a stay-at-home order until April 6, so I am working from home. For the most part, I am OK with that, but I worry about Mle demanding my attention, as I have said. I pray that we can develop a good system so that I can get work done and not lose my mind. I want the same for Kim.

I'll need to go on a lot of walks as a way of taking a break from the noise and chaos of living with so many people, most notably a four-year-old I cherish beyond words but find exhausting.

The number of people in the US testing positive with COVID-19 topped 100,000 today, and the number of deaths in the US is over 1,500. A colleague of mine, a biology professor who specializes in cell biology, emailed me a graph projecting that the pandemic will peak in the US around April 14 and that, by August, about 84,000 Americans will have died. I hope that is a gross overestimate.

Over 9,000 have died in Italy, and I think over 5,000 have died in Spain. Countries all over the world are on varying degrees of lockdown.

I wrote a poem for my students to indicate how much I miss being with them in person. Here it is:

Your absence haunts the halls on the Hill.
You are on the other side of my keyboard.

I miss trying to make you laugh in person,
Learning with you in person,
Wearing ridiculous socks in person,
Seeing your faces, hearing your voices in person,
Revising and brainstorming and editing in person.
In person—why I went into teaching.

We will manage online.
Online can be effective.
But when it is forced,
The absence of "in person"
Is ever present,
Haunting.

I can't wait for the reunion
That someday will surely come.

I made it easily accessible so that the message was unambiguous. I hope they found it comforting, edifying, or something positive. I want them to know how important they are to me, to all of us on the Hill.

We may not be meeting in person, but we are still a university. The university is the people, not the buildings (just like the Church).

In the lazaretto portion of the Italian journal, Seton includes what looks like a poem, or maybe a text to a hymn. It does not appear to be one of her own, although she did write a good bit of poetry. Here is the text she includes on November 25 (I have copied it exactly as it appears in *Collected Writings*, volume I):

"Though torn from Natures most endearing ties,
"The hearts warm hope, and love's maternal glow
"[Though sunk the Source on which the Soul relies]
"[To soothe thro' lifes decline its destin'd woe]
"Though Sorrow still affecting ills prepares
"And o'er each passing day her presence lowers
"And darkened Fancy shades with many cares
"With many trials crowds the future hours
"Still in the Lord will I rejoice

Friday, March 27, 2020

"Still in my God I lift my voice
"Father of Mercies! still my grateful lays
"Shall hymn thy name, exulting in thy Praise[1]

A footnote in *Collected Writings* indicates that the complete verses are found elsewhere in Seton's writings, but the source of this text is unknown. In any event, the text is typical Seton in its hopeful honesty. While it is open about life's difficulties, such as in the line "Though Sorrow still affecting ills prepares," it is ultimately trusting in God, such as in the line "Still in my God I lift my voice." Such a sentiment is typical of the Psalms, which Seton was fond of, as well as of many other hymns, some of which she surely knew. Indeed, throughout her life, Seton readily quoted Scripture and hymns, among other sources.

Her use of this poem or hymn during quarantine and my writing of a poem during the pandemic remind me of our tendency as humans to draw upon poetic language to help us through challenging times. The crisis rises before us, and one way we cope is by summoning the compressed, emotive, evocative, imagistic language and rhythms of poetry. Such writing helps us at least to inch closer to expressing what may at first seem inexpressible, the emotions we feel in response to a painful hardship. Actually, in a broader sense, the entire Italian journal is a literary attempt to capture the emotions and plights of a perilous ordeal, a time of sharp grief and anxiety for Seton. And repeatedly, as I am aiming to show throughout this book, she manages to be eloquent, poignant, and wise in her writing (much more so, frankly, than this passage she quotes).

Indeed, one of my larger points in writing this book is that Seton's journal is a poetic, literary work that can help us through this time of coronavirus by bestowing upon us words at their most intense and potent that facilitate our ability to express our emotions and articulate our ordeals.

1. Bechtle and Metz, *Collected Writings*, vol. I, 259–60.

13.

Saturday, March 28, 2020

Katie at the Hospital

Katie works as a security guard at the hospital, where she regularly comes in contact with coronavirus patients. Last night, one was combative. She had to wear special gear to handle him. When she got home, she hurried off to shower and put her clothes in the wash before spending time with us.

She is not a health care worker. I do not mean to take away from what health care workers are doing now, how they are sacrificing their safety for the sake of others (even more than they normally do). My sister Susan, who lives in Arizona, is one of those health care workers. But Katie also deserves credit because she, too, is risking her safety to keep the rest of us safe. And she does it for mediocre pay and often goes unappreciated. Indeed, some of the more hostile visitors and patients at the hospital see her as the enemy.

Thanks, Moo (her nickname), for being one of the many unsung heroes contributing to guiding us through this long, relentlessly building nightmare.

According to the graph that my colleague gave me, which is from the Institute for Health Metrics and Evaluation (IHME), it is predicted that around 542 people will die today.

I want all of this to end now.

14.

Thursday, April 2, 2020

Depression

Depression has hit me hard these past couple of days, just as it often afflicted Seton, particularly when she was young (when she was eighteen, she wrote a poem in which she contemplates suicide). I'm slightly inclined toward depression anyway (I've taken medication since 2002), and a pandemic doesn't help. The death rate is increasing significantly. So far, 5,137 Americans have died, 48,320 people worldwide. By the end of today, we will likely have over 6,000 deaths in the US. Over six million Americans filed for unemployment last week. And all of this is supposed to get much worse in the next couple of weeks.

Adding to my depression is missing my job, missing Seton Hill. The students, the colleagues, that beautiful, friendly, intellectually stimulating, social justice-oriented, lovely world of Seton Hill—I grieve its physical absence.

Then there are family challenges. My family is wonderful, but it is difficult being together so much of the time and with so little to do in terms of entertainment and recreation. We go for a lot of walks, and we play with Mle in various ways around the house while also trying to squeeze in bits of schooling. She continues to lash out at all of us lately by yelling, defying us, hitting us, and throwing things. We are unsure why. It may be that she senses that the world is a mess. It may be that we are doing something wrong. I don't know. I feel sad for her, and I feel frazzled, overwhelmed, like a failure.

I hate all of this, yet a small, dark, perverse part of me is thankful for the pandemic. I am thankful because it lets me off the hook for various responsibilities that, honestly, I was both excited about and found daunting. Like traveling to Kansas for work and traveling to Italy to teach students abroad and traveling to Arizona for my nephew's wedding. I love all of those activities, but not having to do them, at least for now, is a relief, honestly.

I also have a twisted, but probably very common, fascination with the horror of all this. The climbing number of deaths, the desperation. Don't get me wrong. I hate that so many are suffering. 99 percent of me wants this to end now. But 1 percent continues to obsess over it with a sick fascination.

That's normal, right? We humans have long found horror and tragedy engrossing. Our entertainment is full of such things.

But basically, I far more want this to end than not.

This nightmare does get me thinking anew about what I want to spend my short time on Earth doing. A colleague (no one at Seton Hill) has persisted in goading me to help with a project of his for which I simply have no interest. I have finally mustered up the courage and resolve to tell him, "No, thank you." I have other projects, other foci, other obligations that I need to devote attention to or would rather concentrate on.

When there's an invisible virus prowling, you rethink how you spend your time.

15.

The Other People of the Lazaretto

Seton was ever devoted to others, even while valuing time alone for prayer, reading, and meditation. She was no recluse or hermit. When she became a nun, she did not retreat to a cloister. She was not Julian of Norwich, an anchoress who spent decades in one room. Such reclusive people are of great value, but Seton was not one of them. She was relational, including in the lazaretto.

Of course, she didn't have much choice. She was confined to a prison with her husband and daughter. Even so, she embraced the opportunity to care for them. Also, she often writes affectionately of their visitors.

Since I've already written about Anna and William, I will now turn the spotlight to some of the secondary "characters" in her journal.

There are several. There is Captain O'Brien, the captain of the *Shepherdess*, and his wife, who showed concern for the Setons. There is an older man named Louie who waited on the Setons in the lazaretto, including by cooking for them. One time he brought them flowers. There is also Guy Carlton Bayley, Seton's half-brother, who was working for the Filicchis and who visited the Setons and tended to them in the lazaretto. Seton writes that he was like an angel.[1]

1. Bechtle and Metz, *Collected Writings*, vol. I, 258.

One night, survivors of a shipwreck were brought to the lazaretto. They were noisy and restless. Anna compared their noisiness with her family's peace. Seton agreed and assured Anna that she would see "many more such mysteries."[2]

And, of course, there were the Filicchis. There were the brothers, Filippo and Antonio. Filippo, the elder brother, was married to an American, Mary Cowper. The couple had no children. Antonio was married to Amabilia, and they had ten children. The Filicchis became connected to the Setons when Filippo met William while spending time in the United States. William then traveled to Italy in 1788 with Filippo and thus met Antonio (William married Elizabeth in 1794). William formed an enduring friendship with the Filicchis, and, later, so did Elizabeth. I will say more about them later.

One secondary figure in the Italian journal who was especially prominent and important was the Capitano, or, as Seton often calls him, "Our Capitano." He underscores several important themes of the journal.

The Capitano was a captain in the Italian military who was guarding the lazaretto. He inspired a largely positive response from Seton. He oversaw the Setons's initial transition from the ship to the lazaretto. He often showed them compassion. On their first day, for instance, he sent them "3 warm eggs, a bottle of wine and some slips of Bread."[3] On Monday, November 21, the Capitano set up a bed for William and curtains provided by the Filicchis, as well as benches for Seton and Anna to lie on. Seton reports that the Capitano spoke to them with "a voice of kindness" that encouraged her to look to "le bon Dieu."[4] She notes that in the Capitano she "found every expression of a benevolent heart."[5] She describes him as having gray hairs and "a kind and affectionate countenance."[6] He shared with Seton that he had had a wife whom he loved and who gave him a daughter but then died—suggesting that the cause of death was

2. Bechtle and Metz, *Collected Writings*, vol. I, 261.
3. Bechtle and Metz, *Collected Writings*, vol. I, 252–3.
4. Bechtle and Metz, *Collected Writings*, vol. I, 256.
5. Bechtle and Metz, *Collected Writings*, vol. I, 256.
6. Bechtle and Metz, *Collected Writings*, vol. I, 256.

complications from childbirth. Seton writes that the Capitano then "clasped his hands and looked up—and then at my W[illiam] 'If God calls what can we do, et que voulez vous Signora [What do you wish, Madame?].'" She concludes her description of this encounter with the statement, "—I began to love my Capitano—."[7]

This scene is noteworthy for at least two reasons. First, it shows Seton receiving compassion from the Capitano and her responding with affection, thus illustrating the journal's theme of Seton finding God and the sacred among others. Second, and more striking, is that Seton responded positively to the Capitano even though he appeared to imply that William had a good chance of dying. He spoke with love for his wife, who had died and then, according to Seton, looked at William and basically suggested that God may allow William to die and that Seton must accept that. It is intriguing that, as he made this statement of resignation, he shifted to, not Italian, but French, in which Seton was fluent. Was he trying to hide what he was saying from William? If so, then why not shift entirely to French? Was he simply quoting a well-known French saying? Actually, *Signora* is Italian, so he was mixing languages. My guess is that "*que voulez vous*" was a saying, like "*que sera sera*," for the Capitano ended up saying this to Seton on several occasions (A French colleague of mine agrees with my interpretation.). In any case, he suggested (according to Seton's perception) that William very well could die and that Seton needed to trust God's will on that point.

She did not respond to his sober pronouncement with sadness but by writing that she began to love "my Capitano." She did not take offense at the Capitano suggesting that her husband may die. I suspect this response is due to the fact that Seton was already fairly certainly that William would not survive and that she appreciated the Capitano's sharing of his own experience with grief coupled with a faith in God (hopeful honesty) that would have resonated with her.

The next day, " . . . our Capitano who now seemed to understand me a little—again repeated 'I loved my wife—I loved her and

7. Bechtle and Metz, *Collected Writings*, vol. I, 256.

she died et que voulez vous Signora.'"[8] Curiously, she writes this immediately after reporting that William was actually feeling better that day and had received a positive visit from Dr. Tutilli, an Italian physician whom the Filicchis had retained. Perhaps, despite the encouraging news, Seton was still mentally preparing herself for her husband's death and so valued the Capitano's words of love and acceptance. The "now seemed to understand me a little" comment may indicate that the Capitano did not know much English but was learning to comprehend Seton better.

While being compassionate, the Capitano also made sure that the Setons honored the quarantine. For instance, on Wednesday, November 23, when friends, probably the Filicchis, visited William and he, "in eager conversation" ventured "too near," the Capitano used a stick to remind William to keep his distance.[9] Seton did not express displeasure at the Capitano doing this, although she does recall that their situation reminded her of "going to see the Lions,"[10] implying that they were like caged, dangerous animals.

She did not always agree with the Capitano. On Friday, November 25, she writes that he asserted that "all religions are good" and that treating others as you wish to be treated was "the only point" of "all religion."[11] Seton asked if he took this point as a "good principle only or also as a command,"[12] and the Capitano responded that it was a command. Next, she declared that the one who gave that command, God, commanded that the first principle should be to "love the Lord your God with all your Soul,"[13] so shouldn't the Capitano have that be his first principle and not the Golden Rule? The Capitano replied, "Ah, Signora it is excellent—mais il y a tant de choses,'"[14] which is French for "But there are so many things," suggesting that the Capitano struggled to put God first. Seton laments,

8. Bechtle and Metz, *Collected Writings*, vol. I, 256–7.

9. Bechtle and Metz, *Collected Writings*, vol. I, 257.

10. Bechtle and Metz, *Collected Writings*, vol. I, 257.

11. Bechtle and Metz, *Collected Writings*, vol. I, 260.

12. Bechtle and Metz, *Collected Writings*, vol. I, 260.

13. Bechtle and Metz, *Collected Writings*, vol. I, 260.

14. Bechtle and Metz, *Collected Writings*, vol. I, 260.

"—Poor Capitano! Sixty years of age—and yet to find that to give God the Soul interferes with 'so many things'—."[15] She underscores this point in the next line when she quotes that "'. . . the Sinner a hundred years old shall be—lost.'"[16] While some scholars have suggested that Seton is being testy or sharp with the Capitano, I see no evidence of that, and neither, it appears from his response, does the Capitano.

Actually, one of my students proposed that this exchange foreshadows Seton's shift to Roman Catholicism. By suggesting an openness to other belief systems, the Capitano may be functioning literarily as a prefigurement of Seton needing to be open to Roman Catholicism. Perhaps, my student contended, Seton made a point of highlighting this exchange when editing the journal because she knew the ultimate outcome: her conversion to a different religion.

Thus, we see in Seton's theological discussion with the Capitano her continued compassion for him due in part to his failure to understand Christian theology as she saw it. Indeed, repeatedly in her life Seton was welcoming and accepting while also being unwavering in her theology. My students sometimes want to view Seton as accepting of everyone no matter what, but she had her limits when it came to theological beliefs. In fact, early in her teaching career, she wanted to convert people to her beliefs, although she moved away from proselytizing as she grew as an educator. And she was always willing to show compassion. Seton strove for interpersonal connections, but she also was quick to note differences.

Throughout the journal, Seton regards the Capitano as a sweet man who repeatedly tried to help the Setons and who felt great tenderness for Seton especially, even calling her his "weeping Magdalene,"[17] but, at one point, she indicates frustration with him and, indeed, with the entire situation. On Wednesday, December 14, five days before their release, she writes,

> The dampness about us would be thought dangerous for a person in health, and my Ws. sufferings—Oh well I

15. Bechtle and Metz, *Collected Writings*, vol. I, 260.
16. Bechtle and Metz, *Collected Writings*, vol. I, 260.
17. Bechtle and Metz, *Collected Writings*, vol. I, 270.

> know that God is above. Capitano, you need not always point your silent look and finger there—if I thought our condition the Providence of man, instead of the "weeping Magdalene" as you so graciously call me, you would find me a lioness willing to burn your Lazaretto about your ears if it were possible that I might carry off my poor prisoner to breathe the air of Heaven in some more seasonable place—.[18]

Here, Seton reveals a rarely seen ferocity. She would burn the entire lazaretto down with, it sounds like, the Capitano inside, if doing so meant giving her husband the opportunity to breathe fresh air and thus maybe survive. She clearly thought the conditions in the lazaretto were bad for her husband's health, but she accepted that this situation was God's will, not the "Providence of man," and thus resigned herself to the situation. She did not need the Capitano to keep reminding her to accept God's will.

As a side note, I find intriguing that this is the second time she describes herself as leonine. As I mentioned, when the Capitano made sure that William and visitors did not get too close, Seton compared her family and herself to lions being observed. Now she calls herself a lioness. The image suggests power and danger as well as beauty and majesty, even regality. Her repetition of the image is a small motif underscoring that she regarded her family and herself as ones to be feared because of the threat of disease. But when she calls herself a lioness, she implies a bit more: She had power she could unleash if she wished. The image also suggests a positive regard she had for her family and herself. They were special, powerful, and dangerous.

This entry about the fire and lioness is the last time Seton refers to the Capitano. The portrait, then, she paints of him is of an older man (remember, she was only twenty-nine, and she says he was sixty) who had a kind of simple, trusting faith and who consistently ministered to Seton and her family. He is a reminder throughout the journal of a recurring theme in Seton's life: trusting in God, even when you do not like the outcome. Most of the time, she accepted that principle, but occasionally, she fought it. In this

18. Bechtle and Metz, *Collected Writings*, vol. I, 270.

message, then, we hear the theme of hopeful honesty, and in the relationship, we see the theme of encountering the sacred in others. Finally, literarily, the Capitano functions not only as a reminder of a key theme, accepting God's will, but also, through speaking of his wife's death and suggesting that William is going to die, foreshadows the latter's death. He is a bit like an oracle in his repeated declaration of an important truth and in his prediction of what was likely to come, William's death.

In general, then, Seton recounts numerous people who touched her while she was in the lazaretto, both comforting and sometimes challenging her. These people helped her to be hopefully honest and also fueled her spiritual growth.

Likewise, I think about who in my life touches me and whom I touch, even in this age of no touching. There are the students, always, and my colleagues. There are my neighbors, including our next-door neighbors, who have been steadfastly friendly toward us. There are my siblings and my stepdad, despite the miles between us.

There are also the non-human family members who live with us. Yes, the cleaning up after them and their bawling for food in the middle of the night can be less than fun. And yes, Seaira our greyhound literally hounds me to go for a walk or to be petted or to go out or to be fed. But where would I be without them? Meezer sleeping on my lap, Seaira staring at me with brown-eyed adoration that makes me want to be a better person. Our seven cats and dog offer endless examples of God's grace incarnate, hopeful honesty.

16.

Saturday, April 4, 2020

Masks

Today we will likely reach 8,000 American deaths. The CDC is recommending we wear face masks when out in public, although the president is saying he is not going to wear one.

Today is a bit quieter around the house because Mle is not here. She's with her dad. She's always welcome. I'll always play with her. But I am thankful for time apart.

17.

Monday, April 6, 2020

Mom

We passed 10,000 American deaths today. This week is supposed to be especially brutal in terms of loss of life, although New York is showing improvement. The model that I am using, the one from the IHME, decreased its projection from 93,000 deaths to 81,000. So far, the actual number of deaths is below what the model projects for today, which is that we will reach 12,000 deaths. We are unlikely to get that high, although we may see 11,000. In any case, the deaths are too great.

As Dr. Fauci has said, with modeling you are aiming at a moving target. The point of modeling, it seems to me, is not to be precisely accurate but to offer guidance and warning.

Throughout all of this, I keep imagining conversations with my mother, who died suddenly ten years ago this December. I have a long history of fantasizing conversations. I went through a phase of talking with Emily Dickinson, for example, who would generally just be weird and give me abrasive, cryptic advice on writing. I don't know why Mom, though. Repeatedly I have imagined telling her about this pandemic and seeing her look of shock and hearing her replies of distress and sadness. Maybe I am wishing that she were here to provide comfort and solidarity, or maybe I find solace in imagining informing someone who is unaware of all this. There is something empowering about being the bearer of the news, even if it is surreal and heartbreaking. I am a teacher, after all, and we teachers frequently find pleasure in informing others, even when the lesson is grim.

Mom was a social worker ever concerned about the underdog. She would, of course, find all of this horrifying and heartbreaking. She'd also be decisive and pragmatic as ever. She'd read up on the science and medicine and have many suggestions for how to cope, whether we wanted them or not. And she would call to see how we were doing. I miss that, someone calling to see how I am doing.

Mom could be aggravating. She had a larger-than-life, take-charge personality. When Mom walked into the room, you knew it. She made sure you did. She could be loud and talkative and had strong opinions on just about everything. Her relentless pragmatism made her less skilled at entertaining creativity or daydreams, and her narrow views sometimes resulted in her dismissing alternative views as "ridiculous." For instance, I have a Ph.D. in English, a subject she smugly regarded as foolishly preoccupied with trivial matters such as the "third word on the fourth line" (a favorite mocking phrase of hers that revealed, frankly, how poorly she understood the discipline). At the same time, though, she would be glowing with pride about my Ph.D., as she did about every achievement of her children and husband (my stepdad, not my father).

I wish she were here.

Mother Seton is. She will never replace my mother, but she certainly has become a maternal figure for me. She smiles at me, reassures me, expresses to me great faith in God, shows me her passionate devotion to her children and to educating all children. I can see her, hear her, sitting beside me, speaking with soft, graceful clarity, then leaning in to give me a hug.

18.

Tuesday, April 7, 2020

My First Mask

We are almost at 13,000 American deaths. I wore a mask for the first time today, when I went to Walmart to buy litter and a few other items. Many people were wearing masks, but many were not. Keeping six feet apart is virtually impossible at the store, so I did the best I could. It's like a game, trying to stay six feet apart, like playing *Frogger*, with losing possibly meaning death.

When I got home, I washed my groceries off on the porch with bleach water. I keep thinking that, despite my best efforts, the virus could sneak in. Katie is working at the hospital. Despite her best efforts, the virus could sneak in. It is microscopic, durable, and spreads easily. We do the best we can, but who knows?

What will become of us?

Tonight, I did a face-to-face class online with my gender studies students. I hope I did all right. I don't know. I often feel like I'm doing a lousy job. I feel like I am not paying close enough attention to what my students are saying. I hate that I don't know who's who better. I wish I knew better names and faces. I started off asking each student to tell us where they are from. Then I forgot to keep doing that. Or did I? I'm doubting myself, my mind, my abilities. I hate when I get like this. Help me, God, to get my sanity back.

19.

Thursday, April 9, 2020

Passover

While there is evidence that social distancing is working, we are having the predicted increase in daily deaths. Yesterday, we had over 1,900. Today we will likely see at least 2,000, for a total number of American deaths at around 16,000. Worldwide, we are at around 90,000 dead.

Last evening at sundown marked the beginning of Passover. I have heard people say that, just as the ancient Israelites took shelter against God striking down the firstborn in Egypt, so also we are now taking refuge against a killer. But the comparison is dangerous because, in the case of Egypt, it was God who was killing the first born. The killer here is a virus, not God. I'm guessing that most people who make the connection to Passover are not implying that the virus is God's instrument of death, but I have no doubt there are religious groups who are thinking just that. You can bet that there are Christians and others preaching that this virus is God's wrath in response to something that those folks think is sinful.

Christians. Sometimes, they make me so proud. Other times, they make me cringe.

Then a friend of mine suggested that maybe God was using the virus, not to punish us, but to teach us a lesson. I countered that maybe a more theologically sound understanding is that God is using this virus to help us learn but not that God sent the virus to teach us. In other words, perhaps God is responding to the virus by using it to teach us, for example, to spend more time with one another and focus on what really matters. This theology strikes me as sounder than the idea that God sends terrible things to us in order to teach us.

Or maybe it isn't. I mean, no one really knows what God's relationship to the virus is. What we do know is that are to respond to it by caring for each other, and God wants us to do that. God is all about us caring for each other. That is to be the take-away.

My guess is that Mother Seton would think that the virus was God's will but that God would ultimately help us to prevail and that, in the meantime, we are to care for each other.

Mother Seton, I struggle to agree with all of that.

I struggle with questions of theodicy, as we all do. Why, if God is all-loving and all-powerful, does God allow so much horror and misery? Yes, there's freewill. We humans have the freedom to choose sin. When we do, terrible things happen. We end up in a fallen world. So, maybe God shouldn't have given us freewill. Or maybe God could have given us a modified free will in which we have a choice from an array of options, with none of them leading to ruin.

People often say, "Everything happens for a reason," and, "This is all part of a larger plan." I wince inwardly at both of those sentiments. If "Everything happens for a reason" means that everything that happens is part of that larger plan, then God isn't a very good planner. It's hard for me to imagine a plan that justifies the Holocaust or 9–11 or this pandemic. And wouldn't it be helpful for all of us if God let us in on the plan? Then, maybe we could be more patient and understanding when bad things happen. Good leaders tend to be upfront, transparent, but God is frequently cryptic, opaque. Also, if God is making everything happen according to a plan, then does that mean that we don't have free will and thus the freedom to go against the plan?

You would think that the most powerful and wisest and most loving being in the universe could come up with a better plan. Or, if this is indeed the best plan and I just cannot see it as such because of my fallible human perception, you would think that God, who can do anything, could make the plan comprehensible to my feeble human brain.

While I am not a sophisticated theologian, I do know that some theodicies make out God to be cruel. I hope that God is not cruel at all but is always compassionate and loving and wants us to be the same. Yes, what looks like cruelty to us might be compassion in disguise, but it's hard to see that with a virus that kills thousands of people every day

In the lazaretto, Seton is determined to trust in God, even while she expresses heartache and even the occasional moment of anger or faltering faith. She embraces the ordeal as an opportunity to grow spiritually, to strengthen and prune her soul through prayer, study, meditation, and resolution. She is a pastor to her dying husband, and, in so doing, she merges her spiritual life with her role as wife. She engages in theological discussion with the Capitano. And over and over, she sees God incarnate in the people around her, in nature, in the ringing church bells she could hear from the lazaretto.

I'm not there yet.

20.

Thursday, April 9, 2020

Eucharist

In addition to Passover, today is Holy Thursday or Maundy Thursday, the beginning of the three great days known as the Triduum. These are the holiest days of the year for us Christians because they commemorate the Last Supper and the suffering, death, and resurrection of Christ. Normally, we would be in church a lot these days.

I'm ordained, so we could celebrate Communion at home if my family would like. We don't have wine, but we can come up with a substitute, or I can go buy some grape juice. Come to think of it, Giant Eagle probably has wine. Also, my pastor has posted a service online we can view.

And we can still honor the spirit of the day. It is on this day, for instance, that we remember Christ instituting Holy Communion/the Eucharist, the ritual eating and drinking of bread and wine. For some, such as Roman Catholics and us Lutherans, the bread and wine are the real body and blood of Christ, but for many Christians, there is a more figurative or symbolic understanding. In any case, the ritual is, among other things, one of uniting people to each other and to God as well as a reminder of Christ's suffering, death, and resurrection. The ritual is infinitely more, but it is certainly at least those things. Perhaps, then, we can find more ways to focus on and even reinforce unity with God and each other as well as new ways to remember Christ's sacrifice and victory, since we cannot physically observe Communion.

I just watched the service that the pastor posted on YouTube. It is lovely and reverent. I am grateful. It is also faceless. Neither pastor nor anyone else appears on screen. You only hear his voice and the voice of those present, the handful of people helping with worship (such as the organist), no doubt maintaining a distance of at least six feet from each other. Key texts from the service appear on screen so that we all can follow along. So, there are no faces, and there is no Eucharist, no Holy Communion. Of course, there cannot be. I understand that, but it weights down my heart to observe a Maundy Thursday service that omits the most important part.

Kim, Mle, and I ended up having our own Eucharist this evening. I bought wine and gluten-free matzoh crackers (Kim can't have gluten). I poured a little wine in three tiny glasses and put crackers on a white saucer. The three of us sat at the dining room table. I recited the words of institution and then gave Kim and Mle each a cracker and a glass containing a bit of wine. "The body of Christ, given for you . . . The blood of Christ, shed for you." We had M commune me. She managed the words as best she could. She has participated in the Eucharist many times at church, so she was somewhat familiar. Even though many parents in the Lutheran Church wait until their children are a good bit older before they start receiving the Eucharist, Kim and I decided (and our pastor agreed) to let Mle receive the body and blood. After all, there is no reason why a person has to understand fully what's going on in order to receive the sacrament. Indeed, no one but God understands *fully* what's going on in the Eucharist. Besides, the Orthodox Church communes infants, so we figured it would be fine to commune Mle.

By the way, M is great at praying. This is one way she cares for us, just as Anna cared for Seton in the lazaretto. When we say grace before meals, she insists on leading the prayer, and boy does she. Since she is fascinated with animals and boo-boos and, especially, seeing dead animals along the road, her prayers usually go something like this: "There was a dead deer and a bunny rabbit, and he got bleed, and then he went to the doctor, and so did the squirrel, and there was a little boy who got a boo-boo, and he got bleed, and then they died, and then they went to heaven," followed by a rather lengthy silence before she punctuates the moment with a big "Ahhhhmenn."

Now, I get that this prayer: A. makes no mention of God. Then again, neither do the biblical books of Esther and Song of Solomon. More importantly, I understand that: B. the prayer reflects a preoccupation with death. Mle does indeed ponder death a great deal. It mystifies and intrigues her. We try our best to explain it to her and reassure her that she and all of us in her family are safe. We don't venture into the details of the matter. We just try to explain simply and reassure her.

I appreciate that her prayer seems to imply a concern for others, especially animals, and that she has faith that all the dead go to heaven. Apparently Mle is a universalist. In fact, recently she indicated that a healed boo-boo on her finger had gone to heaven.

Along with praying, she loves playing doctor. Throughout the day, she wears a doctor coat we bought her and uses her toy stethoscopes (which she calls a telescope despite our repeated efforts at correcting her). She checks my heart and my ears and eyes and gives me shots and, of course, the all-important Band-Aid. She does the same with Kim, Katie, the cats, the dog, and stuffed animals, especially Scooby-Doo and Minnie Mouse.

I am thankful on this special Thursday to have a granddaughter who cares about the Eucharist, believes everyone is going to heaven and that death is not the end, and practices foot-washing through taking care of others by playing doctor (She's also eased up on the hitting, thanks be to God.).

Speaking of foot-washing, this day we do indeed remember Jesus washing the disciples' feet, which he did at the Last Supper (according to John's gospel), and then declared that we need to wash one another's feet. He also instituted the *mandatum*, the New Commandment, which is that we are to love one another as Christ has loved us. While the call for us to love one another wasn't new at the time (or probably ever), the newness came from imitating Christ. That loving of one another, washing each other's feet, we can clearly practice, even in this day of social distancing. Indeed, social distancing itself becomes an act of love for others, since, by doing so, we are not only protecting ourselves but one another. By staying away, we draw closer.

Wearing a mask is an even better example, since, for most of us, the homemade cloth masks we use are actually not going to protect us from getting the virus but will protect others from contracting the virus from us. After all, anyone can be a carrier of the virus regardless of whether they show symptoms.

All of this gets me thinking about dear Seton, who, during her quarantine, had to make do liturgically and who often received comfort and encouragement from those around her. Many washed her feet as well as those of her husband and daughter. She, likewise, did plenty of foot-washing herself.

21.

Seton and Worship in the Lazaretto

Ever the devout Episcopalian (remember that she didn't convert to Roman Catholicism until 1805), Seton strove to find ways to maintain her worship life while in the lazaretto. Early in her journal (in an entry dated "November 19," although it sounds like she actually penned this part of the entry the next morning), she writes to Rebecca, "I went to sleep and dreamed I was in the middle Isle [sic] of Trinity Church singing with all my Soul the hymns at our dear Sacrament."[1]

Worship is a major theme in the Italian journal. Seton repeatedly reports singing hymns, praying, and reading scripture and sermons. The nearby ringing church bells, which she mentions often, reminded her that her focus should be on God while also underscoring what she was missing, attending worship, something she finally got to do while staying with the Filicchis.

She even tried to connect with the worship life she had left behind in New York. On Sunday, November 20 (just one day after being confined to the lazaretto), she writes,

> [I]t was 9 oclock [sic] with us—3 at Home—I imagined what I had so often enjoyed and consoled myself with the thought that tho' seperated [sic] in the Body six thousand miles—my Soul and the Souls I love were at the Throne

1. Bechtle and Metz, *Collected Writings*, vol. I, 251.

> of Grace at the same time, in the same Prayers, to one Almighty Father . . .[2]

Similarly, on Friday, December 2, she expresses that she will miss celebrating Christmas back home but then declares that

> one thing is in my power, tho' communion with those my Soul loves is not within my reach in one sense, in the other what can deprive me of it . . . at 5 oclock [sic] here, it will be 12 there—at 5, then in some quiet corner on my Knees I may spend the time they are at the altar, and if the "cup of Salvation" cannot be recieved [sic] in the strange land evidently, virtually it may, with the Blessing of Christ and the "cup of Thanksgiving" supply in a degree . . . Oh my Soul what can shut us out from the love of Him who will even dwell with us through love—[3]

Extraordinarily, she expresses that Christ will unite her and the people back home during worship, especially the Eucharist, even though Seton cannot literally consume it. Christ will give her the Eucharist virtually. Christ's love will unite her with the people back home so that they can still partake of the Eucharist together. Neither distance nor lack of bread and wine for Seton was an obstacle.

This moment illustrates well the theme of encountering God through others found throughout the Italian journal. Seton cared deeply about connecting with others, and she was determined to do it despite the physical and logistical barriers. Her thinking was that Christ enabled her to overcome those barriers so that she could connect with her loved ones. Of course, she had no way of knowing if they were thinking of her at such moments. It didn't matter. She still connected with them.

The moment also illustrates well how much Seton cherished the Eucharist, even before converting to Roman Catholicism and embracing that church's doctrine of Real Presence, the belief that the bread and the wine are literally transformed into the body and blood of Christ at the moment of consecration while retaining the

2. Bechtle and Metz, *Collected Writings*, vol. I, 255.

3. Bechtle and Metz, *Collected Writings*, vol. I, 266.

physical properties of bread and wine. While Roman Catholicism, with its focus on the Eucharist, would intensify and deepen Seton's reverence for the Eucharist, it did not create her reverence. As we can see here and elsewhere, Seton cherished the Eucharist as a Protestant, too.

In fact, on December 24, she presided over her own Eucharist. At this point, the Setons were staying in Pisa, no longer confined to the lazaretto, but William was in "constant suffering."[4] When he expressed a desire for the Eucharist, Seton resolved that "well we must do all we can and putting a little wine in a glass I said different portions of Psalms and Prayers which I had marked hoping for a happy moment and we took the cup of Thanksgiving setting aside the sorrow of time . . . ."[5] Given the dire situation, Seton played the role of priest to offer a makeshift Eucharist for her dying husband. In this instance, she made no mention of the people back home; her focus was on providing pastoral care for her husband. She very well may have thought that this was his final Eucharist.

This moment epitomizes two features of Seton that would recur throughout her life. First, we see her flexible pragmatism. The situation called for her to preside at the Eucharist, so she did. Second, we see once again her willingness to step into a role normally reserved for a man. Years later, as the mother of the Sisters of Charity, she did her best to respect her male church superiors. Indeed, some of them she came to depend on heavily, such as Father Simon Bruté, who eventually administered her viaticum (final Eucharist before death). At the same time, she was not be afraid to challenge the male leadership, such as when she expressed to Bishop Carroll her displeasure with Father John David.[6] As I mentioned, Joan Barthel, in her biography of Seton, calls her a feminist. That might be a bit of an overstatement; she often submitted willingly to male authority in a patriarchal church. However, she was not opposed to challenging that authority in the name of serving God and people in need. Indeed, when she finally returned home to New York, she

4. Bechtle and Metz, *Collected Writings*, vol. I, 273.

5. Bechtle and Metz, *Collected Writings*, vol. I, 273.

6. Barthel, *American Saint*, 141–42.

parted ways with her beloved Episcopal priest, John Henry Hobart, by deciding to convert to Roman Catholicism, a move that painfully estranged the two. This moment on December 24 in the lazaretto of Seton-as-priest for her husband is an early example of that pragmatic flexibility that went against the norm.

I wonder what pragmatic flexibility we will have to do as we live through this crisis. Actually, we have already had to be flexible, such as by learning to work from home and administering Eucharist there. Like Seton, I am generally not defiant. I am obedient and compliant. For instance, I am careful to follow the social distancing guidelines as best I can. One lesson from Seton, though, is that sometimes you need to be flexible for the greater good.

I hope she will help me to know how to be flexible for that greater good.

22.

Friday, April 10, 2020

Good Friday

Good Friday. Jesus's death is the day of greatest death so far in the pandemic. 1,953 people have died today so far. Over 18,000 Americans have died, over 100,000 have died worldwide.

I realize that Jesus's death brings with it hope for new life.

Hope or no hope, death surrounds us.

23.

Saturday, April 11, 2020

Easter Bunny

The final toll for yesterday was 2,074 American deaths, the most of any one day so far. Today we passed 20,000 American deaths. We now have a higher death toll than Italy. We lead the world in death.

This afternoon, the Easter Bunny rode through our neighborhood, Southwest Greensburg, a sweet community of a couple thousand people separate from the city of Greensburg proper. Our little Mayberry-esque neighborhood often tries to do family-oriented activities. Today was one of them. We stood out front of our house on Welty Street with our next-door neighbors waiting in the sunny, brisk air for the bunny. At around four, a mini parade made its way down the street. A police car, a fire truck, then a truck with someone dressed in a white bunny costume. In the name of social distancing, all the members of the parade, including the bunny, stayed in their vehicles, except for a few volunteers. One of them, a tween girl, ran up to the curb and tossed a goodie bag, careful to keep her distance from us. She wore a mask.

24.

Sunday, April 12, 2020

Easter Day

This morning, I participated in the Easter service at Trinity Evangelical Lutheran Church in Latrobe, PA (about twenty minutes from my home). I have known the pastors there for decades and have been involved with that congregation from time to time over my twenty-three years in the area. It's a large congregation with a lovely, well-appointed worship space. The pastors are wise and kind, people of integrity. A few weeks ago, I was asked if I would preach for the Easter Vigil, a service held the night before Easter. When that was cancelled due to the pandemic, I was asked if I would preach the Easter morning sermon for a service that would be live streamed as well as broadcast on the radio. There would be no congregation present, and the seven of us who were present would practice social distancing. I said that I would be honored.

The service went well. Last I checked, it had 4,000 views online. It is the most widely heard Easter sermon I have ever given. More important than the numbers, though, are the positive comments I received. I am thankful that the sermon was edifying and comforting for at least some people.

25.

The Sermon

Roll Away the Stone

Text: Matthew 28:1–10

I want to draw your attention to an important detail in Matthew's account of the resurrection, which I just read for you.

All four gospels, Matthew, Mark, Luke, and John, tell us about that first Easter. All four say Mary Magdalene (and others) went to the tomb early on Sunday morning. All four say that there was some sort of being or beings at the tomb who announced that Jesus had been raised.

However, in Matthew's version, the one we just heard, Mary Magdalene and another Mary, upon arriving at the tomb, experience an earthquake because an angel, descending from heaven, rolls the large stone away from the entrance to the tomb. The angel sits upon the stone and announces that Jesus has been raised. The angel invites the women to look into the tomb to see that Jesus is, in fact, no longer there.

Did you catch that? When the angel rolls away the stone, he reveals that Jesus is already gone. In other words, the angel does not roll away the stone so that Jesus can get out of the tomb. Jesus doesn't need the angel's help. No, the angel rolls away the stone, not to let Jesus out, but to let the women in so that they can see that, in fact, the tomb is empty.

God has the angel roll away the stone so we can see that a place of death is now a place that indicates life, an empty tomb. A place of death, a tomb, is now devoid of death. A place where we would expect to find death infernal is actually a place where we find life eternal. And God has the angel roll away the stone so that we can see.

God rolling away the stone to reveal life where we would expect death—that truth is the beating heart and throbbing soul of Good Friday and Easter. When we look to the cross on Good Friday, it appears to the unguided eye that we are simply seeing a first-century man being tortured and executed by an oppressive empire, but what we are really seeing is God in human form (while still remaining God) saving humanity and the rest of creation. What looks like death is actually life. How can we tell? Because, through Scripture, over and over, God rolls away the stone that blocks our vision. God uses Peter in our reading from Acts 10 and our psalm and Colossians 3 to remove the stone so that we can see that what looks like death, a man dying by crucifixion, is actually life, God-made-flesh saving all of us, justifying us by amazing grace.

It looks like Jesus is just a man being put to death by being hung on a tree, but Acts 10 removes the stone by teaching us that he rose from the dead. God rolls away the stone, rolls away our ignorance, rolls away our fear, rolls away our disillusionment, rolls away our confusion, rolls away our cynicism, rolls away our dread, to show us life where we expected to see death.

Let me ask you, then: How does God call us, the baptized, the saved by grace through faith, to roll away the stones of the world so that we all can see God giving life where we thought there was only death?

Death is indeed all around us. The loss is heart-rending, overwhelming. The world is full of lamentation and devastation. Our rooms are locked for fear of infection. In this time of brutal loss, how can we, God's Easter children, roll away the stones so that we all can see that life is stronger than death, that where we expect only death, we find God bringing us life eternal, hope, salvation?

Of course, we want to take seriously people's grief, heartache, and loss. All of that loss is real and cleaves the soul. We do not want to dismiss or trivialize anyone's pain. We also want to take seriously the guidelines in place that are helping to keep one another and ourselves safe. Rolling away stones does not mean needlessly and foolishly exposing ourselves and one another to danger. But it is Easter, so death does not have the final word. It is Easter. The angel rolls away the stone to reveal life. How can we, like the angel, Spirit-empowered, roll away the stone so that all can see?

One crucial way is by helping people see that God brings healing and love through the kindness of other people. It is easy to grow cynical and think that the world is nothing but cruelty, but we in the Church, through words and actions, can roll away the stone of cynicism to enable people to see that billions around the world are feeding one another with actions and words of compassion. It may look like all we have is death, but there is life. Through our words and actions, we can continually reassure one another that we are all indeed helping each other and that death does not have the final word. Life does. Love does. Hope does. God does.

Another way to roll away the stone is to guide one another to see the good opportunities embedded in this sad and frightening time. Again, I don't want to trivialize or dismiss the pain, but many have written and spoken of the good in the situation. For instance, is it not during crises that we tend to reassess our values and remember what is really important, what really matters? Is it not during crises that we often stop to think, "Oh, right, this is what really matters in life, not all the things I normally fret about"?

Elizabeth Ann Seton, the first American born person to be declared a saint, found herself in quarantine in 1803. She, her husband, and their oldest daughter had traveled from their home in New York City to Livorno, Italy to stay with friends. But when they got there, the Italian government forced them into a month of quarantine out of fear that they might be carrying yellow fever, which was ravaging New York at the time. The Setons had to stay in a lazaretto, a dank, spare facility much like a prison. Elizabeth wrote a journal about that painful time. Repeatedly she writes of tears and frustrations and anxieties, but she also writes this: ". . . my confinement of Body [is] a liberty of Soul which I may never again enjoy whilst they are united . . . ."[1] In other words, while she is

1. Bechtle and Metz, *Collected Writings*, vol. I, 257.

frank about the dark side of her situation, she is also able to see the opportunity for life, growth, renewal. She is hopefully honest. She rolls away the stone.

It is easy to become depressed, fearful, despairing. And those emotions are understandable. This is a profoundly disturbing time. Despair can be a huge stone in front of us. But we, the Church, taught by God, empowered by the Spirit, can roll away that stone of depression and anxiety and cynicism and despair to reveal to one another the compassion, the love, the tenderness, the actions large and tiny and every size in between. Death is painful. There is no denying that. But life is here, amid the death, greater, eternal. After death is a comma, because there is more. There is life, period. Exclamation point.

Throughout the coming weeks, these fifty days of Easter, let's each be attentive to what stones block our view from seeing life and love and resurrection. How can we roll away those stones, such as through video chats or text messages or phone calls or donations of money and goods, to show one another that, while everything may look like death and while feeling sadness and fear is understandable, there is, ultimately, life?

The angel certainly has rolled away the stone for us, sent by God. "Come. See where he lay. He has been raised."

And then, we turn, and there he is. Jesus, with scarred hands, embraces us.

26.

Wednesday, April 15, 2020

Kim's Birthday

Yesterday, we had our highest one-day death toll for the United States, around 2,400, and the president declared that the US would be cutting its funding to the World Health Organization.

Today is the birthday for my wife, Kim. We will be getting takeout from Red Robin and having gifts and cake for her. I am confident that this small celebration will bring us some much-needed joy and levity.

Kim is so dear to me, and I am ever grateful for our nineteen years of marriage. Kim is, as my stepdad once said of her, "constant and concrete." She is constant in that she is ever faithful and dependable. She is endlessly dedicated to her family. She is concrete in that she is a practical doer. She cleans our home diligently, works hard at her job to help low-income people get housing, shows her love for all of us through one thoughtful action after another. Few people are as tirelessly dependable as my wife.

She's also fun. She loves to "play," as she calls it, meaning engaging in small acts of mischief. For instance, occasionally, when I am driving, she will suddenly squeeze my thigh, causing me to jump and squeal (I am pretty ticklish). There is no danger here—she knows that I will not lose control of the car—just mischief.

We also enjoy many hours of just being together. We like the same shows on TV. We both love the beach. We both love cats. We cherish our children and M.

Wednesday, April 15, 2020

We are each other's Chee. "Chee," our nickname for each other, is derived from, well, "furry chicken." You see, we were at a petting zoo years ago, at which there were chickens with feathers on their feet. We thus called the chickens "furry." So, we started calling each other "Furry Chicken," then "Furry Cheeken," then "Cheeken," then "Chee."

I love our nickname. It's distinctive, a little quirky, and reflects our love of animals. It's a warm, intimate nickname. It's us, quintessentially.

If I have to go through a pandemic, I'm glad I get to do it with my Chee.

How heartbreaking that Mother Seton lost her beloved husband, her Chee, during that quarantine. My goodness. I cannot imagine such a loss, and I find astounding Mother Seton's ability to go on with such strength and grace.

I don't think I could go and do likewise.

27.

Thursday, April 16, 2020

Dancing

At last check: 31,590 Americans dead, 140,773 dead worldwide, according to CNN, which cites Johns Hopkins University as its source.

I need a happy thought to help me cope with this death.

Here's a truly happy thought. On this date, April 16, in 2012 (it was a Monday), I participated in a dance competition at my university called "Dancing with the SHU Stars," SHU standing for Seton Hill University. We did this competition for several years before it faded away. It consisted of a faculty or staff member putting together a team of students and performing a dance routine. Judges provided feedback, but the audience determined the winner. In 2012, just a few days after defending my dissertation for my Ph.D. in English Literature and Criticism, I was part of a dance team that included three students: Adele, Emily, and Maddy. We did a routine to the Beyoncé song "Single Ladies." We were in costume, of course, including me in high heels and a long, black wig, which fell off during the performance. My response was to toss it into the audience. We were fabulous. The audience loved us. The judges raved about us. And we walked away with the prize: Walmart gift cards.

I loved every second of that experience. Always a bit of a ham who will do pretty much anything in front of an audience, I relished the spotlight. Even better was spending time with those three marvelous students rehearsing and performing. It was hilarious and touching being with them. To express my gratitude, I bought each of them flowers for the night of the performance. Maddy, Emily, and Adele, wherever you are, I am endlessly grateful.

Seton loved to dance. She doesn't mention doing any in the lazaretto, although she does mention jumping rope and hopping on one foot to keep warm. But she and William, a dashing couple, used to go ballroom dancing at galas of New York's high society. She danced at George Washington's birthday party. Many years after her quarantine, she wrote to her daughter Catherine a warning against dancing as a time-consuming distraction from God while also recalling nostalgically how much she enjoyed it and praising it for being good exercise.

But dancing must have seemed very distant from her in the lazaretto, and, right now, it's hard for me to imagine ever doing anything like that dance competition again. We will, of course. Performances, audiences—all of that will somehow return. Today, though, that return seems an unattainable dream.

Speaking of dreams, I've had some strange ones during this pandemic. Indeed, there are articles online explaining that strange dreams during this crisis are to be expected. After all, we are under great duress. I had one a few weeks ago in which I married an acquaintance, even though she remained married to her husband. This situation was not seen as a problem at all (you know how dream logic goes). Also, we did not marry for love but for some logistical reason. And Kim was not part of the world of this dream, I guess. I was happy to wake up to reunite with her. Actually, I had another dream in which she and I got into a horrible argument. I don't remember what it was about, but I woke up distraught.

I had an unpleasant dream last night, too. I can't remember it, but this morning I had a feeling of unease, at once definite and vague.

I don't know why both of the dreams I remember had to do with my marital status. Kim and I are happily secure in our marriage. We have heard of couples finding difficult this time of forced, prolonged togetherness, but we have been content. We enjoy each other's company, rarely argue, and like many of the same things, including watching lots and lots of *Friends*, a show that is comforting in part because, in that world, there is no pandemic.

I wonder if the dream about marrying my acquaintance had something to do with needing to make strange adaptations during this time of crisis. I wonder if my dream of arguing with Kim had to do with fearing that, during this uncertain period, I could lose or at least jeopardize something infinitely precious to me, my marriage.

I accept that I may have to adapt in peculiar ways, but my marriage is non-negotiable, inviolable, a necessity.

28.

Dreams and Mystical Moments

There is an obvious dream motif in the lazaretto portion of the Italian journal. Let us take a look at these dreams, since they are fascinating and also underscore important themes.

I already noted a couple of those dreams. The journal opens with one in which Seton imagined climbing a mountain and being reassured that a beautiful green hill and an angel awaited her on the other side. She also relates on November 19, the day her quarantine began, a dream about singing hymns at her home congregation of Trinity Church. Thus, early in her journal she establishes the importance of dreams.

On November 22, you may recall, she recounts a dream that little Anna had had:

> "Mamma, I dreamed last night that two men had hold of me to kill me, and as one had struck my Breast with a knife, in that instant I waked, and found myself safe and was thinking so it will be with my Soul, while I am struggling with Death, in an instant I shall awake and find myself safe from all that I feared—but then FOREVER"[1]

Seton then punctuates this quote from her daughter with "—our Jesus!!!"[2]

1. Bechtle and Metz, *Collected Writings*, vol. I, 248–9.
2. Bechtle and Metz, *Collected Writings*, vol. I, 249.

Near the end of the lazaretto portion of the journal, she returns to dreams. Seton recalls that, the night before William's death on December 27, she dreamed, "a little angel with a pen in one hand a sheet of pure white paper in the other—he looked at me holding out the paper and wrote in large letters *JESUS* this tho' a vision of sleep was a great comfort."[3] When she related this dream to William, he was comforted, "very much affected."[4] Then, a few hours before his death, he said, "the angel wrote JESUS—he has opened the door of eternal life for me and will cover me with his righteousness."[5]

She follows that entry with another, which concludes the lazaretto portion of her journal with this paragraph, also about a dream:

> I had a similar dream the same night—the heavens appeared a very bright blue a little angel at some distance held open a division in the sky—a large black Bird like an eagle flew towards me and flapped its wings round and made every thing dark—the angel looked as if it held up the division waiting for something the Bird came for—and so alone from every friend on Earth, walking the valley of the Shadow of death we had sweet comfort even in our dreams—while Faith convinced us they were realities—[6]

So, Seton begins and ends the lazaretto portion of her journal with dreams, both of which, like all the dreams she describes, brought comfort. Even Anna's frightening dream of men assaulting her ended on a comforting note. The message in every single dream is that, despite the difficulties and fears, God will bring Seton and her family to eternal peace. The dreams do not deny the present sufferings, but they do offer hope of eternal life, even if not rescue from the present plight. The dreams, then, exemplify the theme of hopeful honesty.

Dreams are also one of the ways that mystics experience intimacy with God, and such was the case here. These dreams

3. Bechtle and Metz, *Collected Writings*, vol. I, 275.
4. Bechtle and Metz, *Collected Writings*, vol. I, 275.
5. Bechtle and Metz, *Collected Writings*, vol. I, 276.
6. Bechtle and Metz, *Collected Writings*, vol. I, 276.

all connected Seton to God and even helped her to connect her husband to God. The angel imagery, too, is reminiscent of mystical writings, which often feature heavenly beings, such as the angel piercing Saint Teresa of Avila, which Bernini famously depicted in stone.

In addition to these dreams, Seton has several moments in the journal reminiscent of the language of Christian mystics such as Julian of Norwich and Saint Teresa of Avila. One such moment is in the entry dated November 15, just three days before Seton and family arrived at Livorno. She describes a thunderstorm that came at midnight and her response of trusting in God. She writes that "My Soul assured and strong in its almighty Protector, encouraged itself in Him, while the knees trembled as they bent to him."[7] Thus, ever embodying hopeful honesty, Seton simultaneously indicates fear and faith.

Next, she writes this intriguing, poetic, somewhat cryptic statement: "—the worm of the dust <shaking> writing at the terrors of its Almighty Judge—a helpless child clinging to the Mercy of its tender Father—a redeemed Soul Strong in the Strength of its Adored Savior—."[8] Such statements, with their imagistic language, intense emotion, and expressions of confidence in God, bring to mind the writings of the mystics.

Nowhere in her journal is Seton more mystical than in her entry on December 1, which comes about halfway through the lazaretto portion of the Italian journal. She opens by describing a peaceful predawn scene with the moon shining and "not a breath of wind."[9] She goes on,

> . . . [E]very thing around at rest except two little white gulls flying to the westward towards my Home—towards my loves—that thought did not do—flying towards Heaven—where I tried [sic] to send my Soul—the Angel of Peace met it poured over the Oil of Love and Praise, driving off every vain imagination and led it to its Savior and its God—"We Praise Thee O God"—the dear strain

7. Bechtle and Metz, *Collected Writings*, vol. I, 247–48.

8. Bechtle and Metz, *Collected Writings*, vol. I, 248.

9. Bechtle and Metz, *Collected Writings*, vol. I, 263.

> of praise in which I always seem to meet the Souls I love and "Our Father"—These two portions are the Union of love and Praise in them I meet the Soul of my Soul.—at ten oclock [sic] read with W. and Anna—at twelve he was at rest—Ann playing in the next room—alone to all the World, one of those sweet pauses in spirit when Body seems to be forgotten came over—[10]

In this extraordinary passage, Seton responds to two gulls flying in the direction of her home in New York to create an image of "the Angel of Peace" that pours "the Oil of Love and Praise" over it, thus enabling her to put aside "vain imagination" and connect with God. She goes on to recall a hymn, "We Praise Thee O God," which helps her to achieve unity. She writes, "These two portions are the Union of love and Praise in them I meet the Soul of my Soul."[11] This rich imagery coupled with a focus on unity with God has a strong mystical quality. Then she punctuates this scene with the statement that, during this time of spiritual solitude and peace while William rested and Anna played in the next room, she experienced "one of those sweet pauses in spirit when Body seems to be forgotten came over me—."[12] The forgetting of the body underscores the mystical nature of this entry.

She continues this mystical inclination in the next part of that entry, in which she shifts to a flashback to her childhood. She recalls the year 1789, the year she turned fifteen, when her father was in England—he often was away due to his work as a renowned physician—and she spent time in the woods. She found a chestnut tree with a bed of moss under it that she sat on. The sky was blue, the sun shining, the flowers fragrant. In that moment, she was "filled with even enthusiastic love to God and admiration of his works."[13] Throughout her life, Seton, like many of us, found God in nature. During the quarantine in 1803, the weather and the ocean likewise led her to God, although, when the weather was violent and the

10. Bechtle and Metz, *Collected Writings*, vol. I, 263–64.
11. Bechtle and Metz, *Collected Writings*, vol. I, 264.
12. Bechtle and Metz, *Collected Writings*, vol. I, 264.
13. Bechtle and Metz, *Collected Writings*, vol. I, 264.

ocean tempestuous, she responded by either being reminded of God's capacity for wrath or by turning to God for safety from such threatening forces.

In any case, as she recollects that halcyon day in 1789, she avers that "still I can feel every sensation that passed thro' my Soul—and I thought at that time my Father did not care for me—well God was my Father—my All."[14] Throughout her childhood, she felt her father's absence more than his presence, but she found comfort in God's never-failing closeness. Her longing for interpersonal connections with her father she replaced with an interpersonal connection with God.

She goes on to share that, back in 1789, she ". . . layed [sic] still to enjoy the Heavenly Peace that came over my Soul; and I am sure in the two hours so enjoyed grew ten years in my spiritual life."[15] What a remarkable statement. Again, the intense communion with God that accelerated her spiritual maturation was mystical in its rich imagery and focus on intimacy with God.

She then connects this 1789 flashback to her plight in 1803: "Well, all this came strong in my head this morning when as I tell you the Body let the Spirit alone . . . with my head on the table lived all these sweet hours over again, made believe I was under the chestnut tree—felt so peaceable a heart—so full of love to God."[16] She draws from her imagination, which she does throughout the journal, to heighten her devotion to God. A key feature of mystics is their tremendous creativity that helps them, likewise, to focus on intimacy with God. Seton underlines this concentration on holy intimacy in this passage when she indicates that she "[dwells] with delight on the hope of all meeting again in unity of Spirit, in the Bond of Peace, and that Holyness [sic] which will be perfected in the Union Eternal—the wintry storms of Time shall be over, and the unclouded Spring enjoyed forever—."[17] Seton draws from her memories, nature, and her imagination to achieve a closeness with

14. Bechtle and Metz, *Collected Writings*, vol. I, 264.

15. Bechtle and Metz, *Collected Writings*, vol. I, 264.

16. Bechtle and Metz, *Collected Writings*, vol. I, 265.

17. Bechtle and Metz, *Collected Writings*, vol. I, 265.

God that looks toward the ideal of eternal divine union that will include "all."

She concludes the day's entry by writing of freedom that comes while imprisoned (another expression of hopeful honesty), a theme we encounter multiple times in the journal: "So you see, as you know, with God for our Portion there is no Prison in high walls and bolts . . . for this freedom I can never be sufficiently thankful . . . ."[18] This mystic's connection to God liberated her from the physical confines of the lazaretto.

Thus, on December 1, Seton writes with the intensity and imagery of a mystic and also longs for interpersonal connections, in the process demonstrating her literary talent. This day is rich with poetic language that stirs both head and heart.

18. Bechtle and Metz, *Collected Writings*, vol. I, 265.

29.

Sunday, April 19, 2020

Teach Peace

Starting this evening at eight PM, every employee and customer at an essential business in PA must wear a mask. Fortunately, I am ready. Katie got me a lovely mask with the words "Teach Peace" on it such that the two words share the "eac," with "Teach" above "Peace."Funny, I hadn't noticed this initially. I thought the mask just said "Peace." Then the cashier at a store, a young man, read the mask aloud, and I got it. Silly *moi*.

That same cashier also said that, at first, he thought my mask had the word "impeach" printed on it, so he launched into a short rant about how "everyone" wants Governor Wolf impeached because he was "five weeks behind everyone else" regarding tending to the coronavirus crisis. This was all news to me. The United States in general was behind-the-ball on the crisis, but I don't know that our state has been any more behind-the-ball than anyone else. Maybe. I'm not saying the cashier was wrong. I'm just saying I don't know.

Today we reached 40,000 deaths.

Dotting the nation are protests against stay-at-home orders, the ostensible argument being that such orders are a violation of our freedoms. I suppose they might be to a small extent, although the rights of others are violated when they are exposed to people who refuse to wear masks. The point of the orders is to protect everyone so as to minimize the number of people getting sick/dying from this virus. Maybe we need to sacrifice a bit of our freedoms temporarily for the sake of the common good.

There have been several faulty comparisons regarding this virus. The big one is to compare this to the flu and argue that, since the flu takes more lives each year than this virus will (maybe?), we therefore shouldn't be taking all these precautions. I understand that none of us wants to have these restrictions, and we are worried about the long-term impact, including economically. But: A. This is deadlier than the flu; B. It appears to be more contagious; C. We don't know nearly as much about it as we do the flu; D. We don't have a vaccine for it.

Then Dr. Phil made the amazingly flawed statement that car accidents and swimming pools kill far more people than this virus, but, he argued, we don't shut down the world for them. But if car accidents and swimming pools were highly contagious, then perhaps we would. A man who prides himself on tell-it-like-it-is common sense displayed a stunning lack of it in that moment.

It's easy to get frustrated with all the stubborn defiance of the stay-at-home and other social distancing orders that are intended to keep us safe. Maybe I am naïve—I have certainly had my moments—but it seems to me that the orders are indeed there to protect us and that we should, therefore, comply with them. Of course, it is easy for me to comply given that I can still work remotely and that I have all my basic needs met and then some. My privilege sometimes blinds me to the plights of others.

30.

Cave Nation

The defiance of social distancing and other practices reminds me of the general polarization of our nation. There are at least two Americas. One is more progressive and celebrates diversity and inclusion. All are welcome to this nation of immigrants, and we should work together to lift one another up. The other America is fearful of change and inclusion, a nation of immigrants that fears immigrants. This other America tends to think there was a Golden Age, usually seen as the 1950s, when everyone knew their place and people went to church and loved Jesus. "Girls were girls, and men were men," to quote the ironic theme song of that trenchant sitcom, *All in the Family*.

Of course, there are really gradations among these two Americas, aren't there? For instance, someone might be supportive of their LGBTQ friends while being opposed to immigration. So, that person is inclusive in one regard, exclusive in another.

Many of us recognize that there is a need for dialog among Americans who disagree. We are great at yelling at each other on cable news and social media. Heaven knows, we Americans love, absolutely love, hurling death threats at people who disagree with us. We also tend—and I am guilty of this—to surround ourselves with like-minded people. Liberals tend to watch and listen to news sources with a liberal bent, while conservatives tend to watch and listen to news sources with a conservative bent.

We have become a cave nation, that is, a nation in which every person lives inside a cave that echoes back to him/her/them what they believe. Maybe some of us are in the same cave, but we are all just echoing back to each other what we want to hear. We need to venture outside our caves and talk to each other, but we are afraid to, so we don't. It's more comfortable to hide inside the cave.

At the university, we try to help students learn how to talk with each other civilly, open to different perspectives, try to nudge people outside of their caves.

I need to work on that more myself. To that end, I read multiple news sources, including ones that are socially and politically at odds with my views. But am I really being open, or am I just checking in with those news sources so that I can tell myself that I am open?

I have certain positions on which I am never budging. For example, I will always work for gender and racial equity.

At the same time, I want to hear opposing views for at least two reasons. First, opposing views sometimes help me to see the cracks in my thinking and thus where I need to strengthen it. Second, listening—really listening, without an answer coiled to strike—can lead me to understand better a different perspective. Greater understanding can then help to foster greater harmony.

But can the nation as a whole break out of the caves, and what can I do to help? On the whole, especially this year, it seems we are stuck in those caves, and that we are going to echo ourselves to death.

31.

Wednesday, April 22, 2020

Earth Day

Earth Day. One outcome of the pandemic is that we are all driving less, so the environment is likely to benefit. Then again, I learned that what we save by driving less we make up for with increased garbage in the form of masks, etc. Can we learn anything from this experience so that we can be better toward the environment?

This is such an important issue for us at Seton Hill. Mother Seton revered nature, and the Sisters of Charity are committed to better care of the planet, which is a key component of Catholic social teaching. Indeed, Pope Francis, in his 2015 encyclical, *Laudato si'*, challenges the entire world to work with greater urgency toward taking better care of the non-human natural world, every giraffe and little bird. The clock is ticking; we are two minutes from midnight.

The pandemic shows us that, when we really, really want to, we humans can make major changes quickly. So why don't we do that regarding climate change?

On another note, many of those changes, which I embrace, nevertheless strike me as strange. Wearing a mask certainly is. My glasses fog up, I become more keenly aware of my breathing and of my sense of otherness. Masks also accentuate people's eyes while making everyone a bit mysterious. It's amazing how hard it can be to recognize a familiar face when you can't see the bottom half of it.

It's hard not to judge people who are not wearing a mask. I wonder why they are not wearing one. Many in the store have a mask on but wear it below the nose, and some wear it below the nose and mouth. As one of my colleagues quipped, "I see lots of protected chins." Are people being defiant, or do they have a good reason? Should I report them? Should I say something to them? I don't do either. I just keep going, right or wrong. Is that unethical or cowardly of me?

I never thought I'd see widespread mask-wearing in the United States. I always found troubling images of widespread mask-wearing in China and gave thanks that we didn't have to do that here.

Another strange feature of social distancing is all the avoidance. When I walk through the store, I try as best I can to dodge to avoid getting close to people. I also tend not to make eye contact. I'm not sure why. It's as if I think just looking at a person might send the wrong message, one of wanting to draw closer or of not respecting social distancing. No, I know what it is. I look away to reduce the likelihood that we might breathe or sneeze or cough in each other's direction. Even though we are wearing masks, I still look away. After all, the masks don't block everything.

Then there is not being able to smile at people. Occasionally, when I do find myself making eye contact with someone, I will smile anyway, in the hopes that it will register in my eyes or another aspect of my upper face. We can generally hear smiles over the phone; perhaps we can sense them despite the mask.

The silence is strange, too. Normally, I love silence. I usually find the world too noisy and so find silence soothing. Too much noise almost hurts me physically. But imposed silence has a slightly eerie quality. When I attend virtual meetings, for instance, the practice is for each person to mute their microphone unless speaking because having all the microphones on causes feedback. So, for most of the meeting, we all have red, crossed out microphone icons in the lower left corner of our screen, and we cannot hear each other. I sit there, in my room by myself, muted, connected with these people in this thin, distant, haunting way.

Seeing crowds has become strange. It is now a bit unsettling to watch movies or videos or anything featuring a crowd of people, or even just a few people. I have gotten so used to avoiding close contact with people except my family that the thought of renewing close contact with others outside my family is disturbing. How can people be together and not worry about getting each other sick? Don't get me wrong. I want to end social distancing, but right now, ending it makes me nervous. It feels menacing.

32.

Thursday, April 23, 2020

Ramadan

Ramadan begins at sundown. It will, no doubt, be challenging during this pandemic, just as everything else is. I pray that Muslims are able to have a blessed Ramadan despite the circumstances.

I get to thinking about how unfairly our nation often treats Muslims, not unlike how unfairly our nation treated Roman Catholics in Seton's day. Sadly, we have a history in our nation of oppressing and demonizing groups and individuals who are not white, Protestant, cisgender, middle- or upper-class, able-bodied, and male. We are also a nation of immigrants that fears immigrants, and a nation that has been built on the abuse, enslavement, and murder of African Americans and the slaughtering and robbing of Native Americans. Understand, there is much that is beautiful and noble about the United States, including our rich, breathtaking diversity. At the same time, we have a horrifying side that responds to diversity with oppression.

We have seen that reality glaring before us during the pandemic. While it has hurt all of us, the pandemic clearly has hurt especially hard the poor and people of color. We have also seen recently in the news shocking yet all-too-familiar stories of white people killing African Americans. Ahmaud Arbery and Breonna Taylor are two recent examples. I pray there are no more.

One of my students asked me what Seton's attitude was toward African Americans. This issue does not come up in the Italian journal, but we know from other sources that the Church, including the Sisters in their early years, benefited from slavery. We also know that the Sisters taught some of the slave children. The student and I agreed that Seton's views regarding race were probably not as progressive as we in the twenty-first century wish they had been.

"But I can say this with certainty," I said to the student, "regardless of Seton's views on race, we know that she stressed love for all people and that the Sisters of Charity and Seton Hill endeavor to be as welcoming and inclusive as possible." Indeed, the Sisters have a long history of working for racial justice and equity. For instance, in the 1920s, the Sisters of Charity of Seton Hill traveled to New Orleans to educate the Sisters of the Holy Family, who were African American and thus were prohibited by segregation to take classes to be certified as teachers. The Sisters of Seton Hill helped those Sisters to be certified.

I pray that this pandemic and the recent acts of violence against African Americans will steer our nation back toward the nobler side of our nature, the side that embraces diversity and equality, and away from our baser side, which fights diversity and equality with every breath. The history of the United States is, in many ways, the history of the struggle between these two sides. May the former prevail.

How many more deaths? Where is all this going?

What will become of us?

33.

Tuesday, April 28, 2020

No Winning

Over 56,000 deaths. Some states, such as Georgia, have begun relaxing social distancing a bit in the hopes of reopening the economy. I get the desire to do that, but the IHME model is now saying there will be more deaths because of those relaxations. There is no winning here. There is just less losing. Economic damage can ruin people's lives, but reducing social distancing too soon or not in the right way could end people's lives.

Personally, I am doing fine. Just worried about what will happen to my beloved Seton Hill in the fall. I've been gaining weight because I have been eating more junk and fewer fruits and vegetables. Back when the university was open, I would go to the dining hall every day and eat a marvelous meal of many fruits and vegetables. Now, it's just harder to get such meals on a regular basis. On top of that, because of stress I find myself taking refuge in Pop-Tarts and chocolate and not in fruits and vegetables. Today, I am renewing my resolve to eat better.

But my little weight struggle is trivial compared to the giant issues facing our nation and the world. Even so, my problems matter to me. I just need to keep them in perspective. They matter, but not as much as the howling crises threatening to devour us.

34.

Friday, May 8, 2020

Graduating Seniors

Today, we had a virtual convocation for seniors graduating with some sort of honor. Since we would normally wear our academic regalia for the event, I wore mine, even though I was just sitting in my office. My whole world is in my office. Other faculty wore their regalia, too.

The event was quite touching. We all participated through Zoom. When it was announced that a student was receiving an award, the student said their name so that the camera would focus on them. It lifted my heart to see their faces and to honor their hard work. So much integrity, brilliance, and hope embodied in our students. Mother Seton was beaming, too.

On Zoom, you can post messages that either everyone can read or that can be sent privately to an individual. I, along with many others, posted effusive congratulations publicly, and I sent quite a few private messages, too. I wanted to hug every single student. I hope we get a chance in August, when our school is planning to do an in-person commencement, which was originally scheduled for tomorrow, May 9.

I'll miss the students. I miss them now. I hate not being with them. They are infinitely precious to me, to all of us on the Hill.

It's a blessing and a bane of the job that you get attached to students and then have to say good-bye to them. We want them to graduate and move on, of course, but we also hate to see them go.

It's even harder when you cannot be in the same room with them.

35.

Saturday, May 9, 2020

Would Have Been Commencement Day

A snowy day, and empty—

36.

Sunday, May 10, 2020

Mother's Day

We almost reached 80,000 American deaths today. The IHME is projecting that over 134,000 will die by August. This number has rocketed up from a prediction of about 72,000 due to the vast majority of states relaxing social distancing practices too soon.

We have many deaths and losses to go before all this ends.

We celebrated Mother's Day by grilling steaks at our house. In addition to Kim, Katie, Mle, and myself, we had over our son, Michael, and the kids' grandmother, whom we call Gram or Gigi. It was a lovely time. Gram brought baked potatoes, salad, and dessert. The meal was minimal work, and we all enjoyed each other's company. We were confident that being together was low risk.

I am thankful for the extraordinary work mothers and other mother-figures do all year round, but especially during this pandemic, when moms have to double as teachers while dealing with the added responsibilities of helping to keep the house clean of the virus and, in general, to keep people safe. Of course, these responsibilities do not fall to moms alone, but let's face it: Our patriarchal society over-burdens moms when it comes to the domestic sphere. So, you know that the pandemic weighs particularly heavily on the shoulders of maternal figures.

How would Mother Seton handle this? I imagine her with me. There she is, sitting on the couch, wearing her signature black cloak and bonnet. This is older Seton, long after the lazaretto, now overseeing her academy and Sisters. She is poised, calm, but also tiny and thin, her health clearly hard on her petite frame. But her large eyes are shining, resolute.

"I'm worried about my family and where we are going with all this," I say to her. I'm seated in my recliner, about ten feet away from her. I want to move to the couch to sit next to her, but I am afraid to get so close to this saintly person. Unworthiness reddens my face.

She clears her throat, pats her chest with one of her hands as she coughs a bit. "I worry, as well, David, while simultaneously I lay my concerns in the lap of Providence. God is our All, and we shall endure through this ordeal."

"I admire your faith," I say, "but what do you do when—" I look away. She is so lovely and approachable that I have trouble looking at her.

Her face brightens. "What do I do when my faith falters?" she asks, correctly guessing my question.

I nod.

"David," she says with a bit of a laugh in her voice, "look at me, dear." I look. She is smiling. "I am not some monster of mischief, nor am I an angel. You need not fear making eye contact with me."

She keeps smiling until I smile back.

She walks over to me and kneels on the floor in front of me.

"What are you doing?" I ask, backing away a bit in my seat.

"Just getting closer so that you can be at ease with me, David." She coughs some more, holding her hand to her mouth. "I do not have all wisdom or all love or all faith, and I certainly have moments when even prayer affords me no comfort, but then I emerge into the light and trust anew in Providence. Lovingly I beseech you to do likewise."

I take a deep breath, her eyes and mine locked. "And what," I finally say, "if I can't?"

She takes my hand in hers. "Keep praying and reading Scripture, even when it seems pointless to do so. And keep helping others. We can always do that, regardless of our faith. And know that I am here with you, helping you and praying for you."

At fifty, I am older than Seton was at her death at age forty-six. Still, she was and is a mother for me.

37.

Tuesday, May 12, 2020

Last Day

Today is the last day of the spring semester. Grades are due at midnight. I hope I served the students well. Will we be on campus in the fall?

American deaths are at about 82,000 and the IHME is projecting 147,000 by August.

38.

After the Lazaretto

Because this book is about quarantine, I decided to concentrate on the part of Seton's journal that she wrote while in the lazaretto, but she was in Italy four months afterward, during which time she and Anna stayed with the Filicchis in Livorno. She and Anna stayed so long because obstacles to their journey home kept cropping up. For example, Anna got sick with scarlet fever, thus preventing them from traveling. Also, their ship, the *Shepherdess*, was damaged by a storm while docked. They eventually arrived in New York on June 4, 1804 on a different ship.

As I mentioned, there were two Filicchi brothers, Filippo and Antonio, and their wives, Mary and Amabilia. Antonio and Amabilia had ten children, although I do not know how many they had at the time of Seton and Anna's stay. The Filicchis were wealthy, and they were devout Catholics, even having a private chapel on their premises.

The Filicchis took her sight-seeing. She spent a week in Florence, for example, during which time she visited museums, including the Uffizi. She also attended the opera with Anna because William had loved that art form, although she ended up hating it.

Most notably, she attended Mass multiple times. The first experience of Mass she recounts is dated Sunday, January 8, when she attended with Amabilia at La SS. Annunziata in Florence. She found the service profoundly moving. She got caught up in the moment, especially the music; she writes, "[I] sunk to my Knees in the first place I found vacant, and shed a torrent of tears at the recollection of how long I had been a stranger in the house of my God, and the accumulated sorrow that had separated me from it."[1] On February 2, Amabilia took her to "Mass as she calls it,"[2] where Seton was overcome by the priest, "the tall pale meek heavenly looking man,"[3] along with the concept of the Real Presence. The experience "gave such strange impressions to my soul that I could but cover my face with my hands and let the tears run."[4]

She eventually fell in love with Roman Catholicism, especially the doctrine of the Real Presence, even to the point of becoming protective of it. In her entry on February 10, she indicates displeasure over a man at worship saying to her at the moment of consecration, "'this is what they call their real *PRESENCE*.'"[5] She writes in response, "—my very heart trembled with shame and sorrow for this unfeeling interruption of their sacred adoration . . . ."[6] She goes on to express bewilderment that someone could not believe in the Real Presence. She no longer saw herself as an outsider observing Roman Catholic worship; she saw herself as identifying with it.

By the time she returned home to New York, she was strongly inclined to Roman Catholicism. In fact, the following March, she converted, even though doing so meant enduring criticism and some ostracism from her Protestant family and heavily Protestant America, although, in the long run, she received support and admiration from family and society alike. Indeed, as the foundress of the American Sisters of Charity of Saint Joseph and one of the pioneers of Catholic education in America, she eventually received the respect and admiration of the world.

1. Bechtle and Metz, *Collected Writings*, vol. I, 283.
2. Bechtle and Metz, *Collected Writings*, vol. I, 289.
3. Bechtle and Metz, *Collected Writings*, vol. I, 289.
4. Bechtle and Metz, *Collected Writings*, vol. I, 290.
5. Bechtle and Metz, *Collected Writings*, vol. I, 291.
6. Bechtle and Metz, *Collected Writings*, vol. I, 291.

39.

Friday, May 15, 2020

Stopping, Not Ending

I wish I could write a tidy ending to this book, but real life rarely has tidy endings.

And, as Lejeune points out,[1] endings are especially tricky in journals. How do you end a journal? You could die, of course. But if you are still alive, how do you decide when to end? There is always more to write. Such is certainly the case here. Why end now? I don't know. Maybe because the semester is over, and my pain through this ordeal, as well as my connection to Mother Seton, is closely tied to the semester. The semester is over, so the journal is, too.

There is no happy ending here. Sure, there is progress. Here, in Westmoreland County, we are transitioning from Phase Red to Phase Yellow, which means the stay-at-home order will be lifted and some non-essential businesses, such as daycare (which always struck me as essential) and retail stores, will be allowed to open. Nationwide, there is a decrease in cases in two dozen states. At the same time, the death toll continues to climb by between 1,000 and 2,000 a day nationwide, and many epidemiologists warn that opening the nation too soon will cause a spike in deaths. And we don't have a vaccine, and the economy is a mess. And the federal administration is curved in on its own self-preservation.

1. Philippe LeJeune. *On Diary*, 187–200.

Friday, May 15, 2020

Regarding Seton Hill, we have successfully completed the academic year. I am proud of how the students rose to the challenge, difficult as it was. I taught well. In general, the semester finished positively, although there has been grieving over not being together, especially among graduating seniors. I pray we can hold baccalaureate and commencement in person in August. I want to shake some hands or bump elbows or whatever we're allowed to do then. Will hugging be allowed?

The pandemic is far from over, just as Seton's troubles were far from over when she was released from quarantine. The end of the quarantine was, by no means, the end of her pain. Her husband died. A month after she returned home to New York, Rebecca, her "soul's sister" for whom she wrote the journal, died. Seton would have great success as a foundress and teacher, but she also would lose two of her children, Anna and Rebecca, before she herself died when she was only forty-six.

The lazaretto portion of the Italian journal, as we have seen, contains much wisdom and encouragement. First, it highlights Seton as one who was honest about struggle while remaining hopeful. Second, the journal shows her growing spiritually, particularly by refining her ability to benefit from hardship and also by helping her to merge her spirituality with her calling as a wife. Third, the journal underscores that we often encounter the sacred in one another. Fourth, the journal showcases Seton's literary talents through exhibiting her use of metaphor and imagery as she reflects on her condition and tells her story. Her journal contains spiritual reflection as well as heartache, joy, anger, and fear. She uses motifs, such as dreams and bells, and she develops characters, such as the Capitano and, of course, her husband and daughter. Her work exemplifies the best of the genre of the diary/journal. Fifth, the journal, through descriptions of dreams and angels and through the expression of Seton's intense closeness to God, has a mystical quality that readers have often overlooked.

I also find Seton's journal has helped me in a personal way to deal with the pandemic. It has helped me, first of all, by giving me empathy. I am not alone: Seton knows what it's like to be restricted due to disease. She also knows what it's like to have to care for others in such close quarters. She works to find a balance between caring for others and tending to her need for spiritual reading, prayer, solitude. She does not ignore those needs because she is too busy caring for others. On the contrary, her spiritual solitude feeds her care for others. So, I want to think anew about how my own need for solitude is not just time to rest and be alone but is also time that can help me to serve better those in need, especially my granddaughter.

Seton's journal also emphasizes the importance of flexibility, even to the point of violating norms of the time. She fills in as pastor to her husband and daughter, even going so far as officiating over a makeshift Mass. Where might I need to be flexible?

In addition, her journal heightens my attention to the spiritual, holy, and even mystical around me. She sees God everywhere: in the storm, in her husband and daughter, in the Capitano, in the tolling of bells. How can I, too, be more attentive to the sacred swirling and clanking, sitting quietly or leaping riotously, tolling or smiling around me?

Finally, I remember that, just as her troubles were far from over after her quarantine, so were her joys, and her legacy of compassion will stretch on forever.

May the same be true for us.

I find great hope, actually, all around me, including in the people and ideals of Seton Hill. Throughout this madness, the students rose to the challenge intelligently and graciously. They met deadlines. They did impressive work. They faced the enormity of the pandemic with grace and tenacity.

Our school motto, which is based on the motto from the Seton Family coat of arms, is "Hazard yet forward." We on the Hill fall back on that motto a good bit. I suppose for some it is a bit hackneyed to default to it, but for me the motto still contains profound truth and hope. The quote does not say that there will not be hazards. It does not promise life will be smooth. However, it does encourage us to proceed forward, to keep going, even when the going gets overwhelming.

40.

Friday, August 7, 2020

The Next Semester

In ten days, we will begin our new academic year. We will be face-to-face, although there will be exceptions for those who are especially vulnerable in terms of health. We will be wearing masks and practicing social distancing. We at Seton Hill are doing everything we can to keep everyone as safe as possible while providing a high-quality education for our students.

As of now, American deaths stand at over 161,000, and the IHME is projecting nearly 300,000 Americans deaths by December 1. We continue to be in a recession, and unemployment is at ten percent. At the federal level, leadership has been unimpressive.

In addition, the nation continues to grapple with its racism, especially in light of the murder of George Floyd on May 25. I have been reading book after book and watching videos and films and attending discussions and panels in order to help me understand better how my words and actions may be contributing to racism and what changes I can make in the name of ending it.

As I think about the start of the semester, I feel a mix of anxiety and excitement. I love, love, love my job, adore the students, cherish my colleagues. Please, God, let this semester go well. Keep us all safe, and help us to provide a solid, rigorous, and supportive experience for our students.

I need to write another book, perhaps one that will focus on how the Filicchi portion of the Italian journal can help us twenty-first-century Americans address racism as we try to stay alive during the worst pandemic in a century.

Pandemic. Racism. Opening the university. Oh, and I think there's some election coming up.

I will keep reading and writing. Really, I have no choice.

And Mother Seton will pray for us.

Indeed, I hear her say, "Fear not, David. *I am*."

Bibliography

Barthel, Joan. *American Saint: The Life of Elizabeth Seton*. New York: St. Martin's, 2014.

Bechtle, Regina and Metz, Judith, eds. *Elizabeth Bayley Seton Collected Writings*. Vol. I. Hyde Park, NY: New City, 2000.

———. *Elizabeth Bayley Seton Collected Writings*. Vol. II. Hyde Park, NY: New City, 2002.

Culley, Margo, ed. *A Day at a Time: The Diary Literature of American Women from 1764 to the Present*. New York: Feminist, 1985.

McGinn, Bernard. *The Presence of God: A History of Western Christian Mysticism*. Vol 6. Part 3. Chestnut Ridge, NY: Crossroad, 2020. xvii.

McNeil, Betty. *15 Days of Prayer with Saint Elizabeth Ann Seton*. Ligouri, MO: Ligouri, 2002.

O'Donnell, Catherine *Elizabeth Seton: American Saint*. Ithaca: Cornell University Press, 2018.

Popkin, Jeremy D., et al., eds. Philippe LeJeune. *On Diary*. Honolulu: University of Hawaii Press, 2009.

Rahner, Karl. *Theological Investigations*. Vol. 20, *Concern for the Church*. Edward Quinn, trans. New York: Crossroad, 1981. Originally published 1961.

Rolheiser, Ronald. "Introduction." John Markey and J. August Higgins, eds. *Mysticism and Contemporary Life: Essays in Honor of Bernard McGinn*. New York: Crossroad, 2019.

www.ingramcontent.com/pod-product-compliance
Lightning Source LLC
LaVergne TN
LVHW010932100826
845153LV00001B/7

* 9 7 8 1 6 6 6 7 0 0 5 8 9 *